FLOWERS FOR
SPECIAL OCCASIONS

FLOWERS FOR SPECIAL OCCASIONS

FIFTY FRESH AND DRIED FLOWER
DESIGNS FOR CELEBRATORY OCCASIONS

TEXT BY
FIONA BARNETT
AND
ROGER EGERICKX

PHOTOGRAPHY BY
DEBBIE PATTERSON

SMITHMARK

THIS EDITION PUBLISHED IN 1996 BY
SMITHMARK PUBLISHERS, A DIVISION OF U.S. MEDIA HOLDINGS INC.
16 EAST 32ND STREET, NEW YORK, NY 10016

SMITHMARK BOOKS ARE AVAILABLE FOR BULK PURCHASE FOR SALES
PROMOTION AND FOR PREMIUM USE.
FOR DETAILS WRITE OR CALL THE MANAGER OF SPECIAL SALES, SMITHMARK
PUBLISHERS., 16 EAST 32ND STREET, NEW YORK, NY 10016; (212 532-6600)

ISBN: 0 8317 3824 3

PREVIOUSLY PUBLISHED AS PART OF A LARGER COMPENDIUM,
THE NEW FLOWER ARRANGER

PRINTED AND BOUND IN SINGAPORE BY STAR STANDARD INDUSTRIES, PTE. LTD.

CONTENTS

· · ·

FLOWERS FOR SPECIAL OCCASIONS

From a luxurious Valentine's posy of deep red roses and an unusual Christmas wreath of clementines and ivy, to lavish bouquets for birthdays and anniversaries, the calendar year presents wonderful opportunities for the flower arranger. Exciting arrangements for weddings, christenings, Easter and Christmas are featured alongside beautiful floral gift-wrappings for every special occasion.

INTRODUCTION
. . .

Right: Golden Wedding Bouquet (page 36)

Traditionally flowers go hand in hand with special occasions – what would a wedding, a christening or a birthday be without celebratory flowers? Throughout the calendar year, from Valentine's Day to Christmas, the flower arranger has opportunity after opportunity to express his or her creativity.

This usually takes the form of a bunch of flowers, but is nonetheless creative for that, especially if you remember that presentation is all. Cellophane (plastic wrap) or tissue paper gift-wrapping will make even the most simple posy of flowers really special, and attention to details such as tying with ribbon or raffia will pay handsome dividends in its effect.

However, it is the big events like weddings which present the flower arranger with the real challenge. The challenge is not just the need for the necessary skills to design, arrange and wire the materials, but also having the skills to organize the project properly by making a series of important decisions correctly.

You must decide exactly what you are going to produce, and calculate the quantities of flowers and foliage necessary. You must avoid buying too much or, worse, buying too little. A carefully considered timetable must be prepared for the event. You must decide when to order the flowers and how long the different varieties will remain in good condition. Remember that some flowers, such as lilies and gladioli, may require a few days before the event to open fully. You must estimate how long it will take to produce each arrangement, headdress and buttonhole. You must consider the time-scale available to you for working with the flowers and, to avoid all-night labouring, how many helpers you will need. Can the large arrangements be made *in situ*, or will they need to be made somewhere else and transported, and if so, how? You must decide what containers, how much plastic foam, and what other sundries you will need.

Clearly, you will need a very long, very comprehensive check-list. And it doesn't even stop there: the participants may wish to have a memento and you will have to consider whether the materials you are using are suitable to preserve. You might even consider the meanings associated with the flowers you are using, so that you can really claim to "say it with flowers".

Above: Orchid Corsage (page 58)

Right: Simple Easter Display (page 27)

The Meanings of Flower and Herb Names

Acacia — *Secret love*
Almond blossom — *Sweetness, hope*
Amaranthus — *Immortality*
Amaryllis — *Pride, splendid beauty*
Anemone — *Withered hopes, forsaken*
Angelica — *Inspiration*
Apple blossom — *Preference*

Basil — *Good wishes*
Bay — *Glory*
Bellflower (white) — *Gratitude*
Bluebell — *Constancy*
Broom — *Humility*
Buttercup — *Childhood*

Camellia — *Excellence*
Carnation — *First love*
Chives — *Usefulness*
Chrysanthemum (red) — *"I love you"*
Clematis — *Mental beauty, purity*
Coriander (Cilantro) — *Hidden worth*
Cumin — *Fidelity*

Daffodil — *Deceitful hopes*
Daisy — *Innocence*
Dianthus — *Divine love*

Evergreen — *Life everlasting*
Everlasting flower — *Unfading memory*

Fennel — *Flattery*
Forget-me-not — *Fidelity, true love*

Gardenia — *Femininity*
Gladiolus — *Incarnation*

Hawthorn blossom — *Hope*
Heartsease — *Remembrance*
Hibiscus — *Delicate beauty*
Holly — *Hope, divinity*
Honesty — *Wealth*
Honeysuckle — *Devotion*
Hyacinth — *Loveliness, constancy*
Hyssop — *Cleanliness*

Ivy — *Eternal fidelity*

Jasmine (white) — *Amiability*
Jasmine (yellow) — *Elegance, happiness*
Jonquil — *"I desire a return of affection"*

Laurel — *Triumph, eternity*
Lavender — *Devotion, virtue*
Lemon balm — *Sympathy*
Lilac (purple) — *First emotions*
Lilac (white) — *Youthful innocence*
Lily (white) — *Purity*
Lily (yellow) — *Falsehood, Gaiety*
Lily-of-the-valley — *Return of happiness*

Magnolia — *Grief, pride*
Marigold — *Joy*
Marjoram — *Blushes*
Michaelmas daisy — *Farewell*
Mint — *Eternal refreshment*
Mistletoe — *Love*

Nasturtium — *Patriotism*

Oak — *Forgiveness, eternity*
Olive branch — *Peace*
Orange blossom — *Purity, loveliness*
Oregano — *Substance*

Pansies — *Love, "Thinking of you"*
Parsley — *Festivity*
Peach blossom — *Long life*
Peony — *Bashfulness*
Periwinkle (blue) — *Early friendship*
Periwinkle (white) — *Pleasures of memory*
Pinks — *Love*
Poinsettia — *Fertility, eternity*
Poppy (red) — *Consolation*

Rose (red) — *Love*
Rose (yellow) — *Jealousy*
Rosebud — *Pure and lovely*
Rosemary — *Remembrance*
Rue — *Grace, clear vision*

Sage — *Wisdom, immortality*
Salvia (red) — *"I am thinking of you"*
Snowdrop — *Hope, consolation*

Sorrel — *Affection*
Southernwood — *Jesting*
Stock — *Lasting beauty*
Sunflower — *Haughtiness, false riches*
Sweet William — *Gallantry*

Tansy — *Hostile thoughts*
Tarragon — *Lasting interest*
Thyme — *Courage, strength*
Tulip (red) — *Declaration of love*
Tulip (yellow) — *Hopeless love*

Violet — *Humility*

Wallflower — *Fidelity in adversity*

Zinnia — *"Thinking of absent friends"*

9

Right: This large-scale harvest arrangement is simple to produce yet has great impact.

Below: The deep red of the roses provides a visual link for these two pretty pots.

BALANCE

Balance is very important in a flower display, both physically and visually. Foremost, the flower arranger must ensure the physical stability of the display. This involves understanding the mechanics of the arrangement, the types and sizes of materials used, how they are positioned and in what type of container. Different types of floral displays require different strategies to ensure their stability.

A large arrangement to be mounted on a pedestal will need a heavy, stable container. The display materials should be distributed evenly around the container and the weight concentrated as near the bottom as possible. Make sure the longer flowers and foliage do not cause the display to become top-heavy.

A mantelpiece arrangement can be particularly difficult to stabilise since the display materials hanging down over the shelf will tend to pull it forward. So use a heavy container and position the flowers and foliage as far back in it as possible.

Check the stability of an arrangement at regular stages during its construction.

Achieving a visual balance in a flower arrangement involves scale, proportion and colour as well as creating a focal point in the display.

The focal point of an arrangement is an area to which the eye should be naturally drawn and from which all display materials should appear to flow. While the position of the focal point will vary according to the type of display, generally speaking it will be towards its centre. This is where the boldest colours and shapes should be concentrated, with paler colours around the outside.

Always think of the display in three dimensions, never forgetting that as well as a front, it will have sides and a back. This is not difficult to remember for a bouquet or a free-standing, pedestal-mounted display, but can be forgotten if a display is set against a wall. Even a flat-backed arrangement needs depth and shape. Recessing materials around the focal point will help give it depth and weight.

Balance in a floral display is the integration of all visual factors to create a harmonious appearance and with practice you will develop the ability to achieve this.

SCALE AND PROPORTION

Scale is a very important consideration when planning a floral display.

In order to create an arrangement which is pleasing to the eye, the sizes of different flower types used in the same display should not be radically different. For example, it would be difficult to make amaryllis look in scale with lily-of-the-valley.

The type of foliage used should be in scale with the flowers, the display itself must be in scale with its container, and the arrangement and its container must be in scale with its surroundings. A display in a large space in a public building must itself be appropriately large enough to make a statement, conversely a bedside table would require no more than an arrangement in a bud vase.

Proportion is the relationship of width, height and depth within a floral display and in this respect there are some rule-of-thumb guidelines worth bearing in mind.

❖ In a tied bouquet, the length of the stems below the binding point should be approximately one-third of the bouquet's overall height.

Below: A wedding bouquet must be in scale with the person carrying it.

❖ In a trailing wedding bouquet, the focal point of the display will probably be about one-third of the overall length up from its lowest point.

❖ For a pedestal arrangement, the focal point will be approximately two-thirds of the overall height down from its topmost point.

❖ A vase with long-stemmed flowers such as lilies, should be around one-third the height of the flowers.

❖ The focal point of a corsage is about one-third the overall height up from the bottom.

However, remember that decisions on the scale and proportion of a floral display are a matter of personal taste and thus will vary from person to person.

The important thing is not simply to accept a series of rules on scale and proportion but to give these factors your consideration and develop your own critical faculties in this area.

Above: This garland headdress utilizes both the colours and scents of summer.

Top left: The heavy blossoms of white lilac are set against the darker stems of pussy willow and cherry.

COLOUR

The way in which colour is used can be vital to the success or failure of a display and there are several factors to bear in mind when deciding on a colour palette.

Though most people have an eye for colour, an understanding of the theory of colour is useful. Red, blue and yellow are the basic hues from which all other colours stem. Red, orange and yellow are warm colours which tend to create an exciting visual effect, while green, blue and violet are cooler and visually calmer.

Generally speaking, the lighter, brighter and hotter a colour, the more it will dominate an arrangement. White (which technically is the absence of colour) is also prominent in a display of flowers.

On the other hand, the darker and cooler the colour, the more it will visually recede into a display. It is important to bear this in mind when creating large displays to be viewed from a distance. In such circumstances blue and violet, in particular, can become lost in an arrangement.

Usually a satisfactory visual balance should be achieved if the stronger, bolder coloured flowers are positioned towards the centre of the display with the paler, more subtle colours around the outside.

Now armed with some basic knowledge of colour theory you can be braver in your choice of palette. "Safe" colour combinations such as creams with whites, or pinks with mauves have their place, but experiment with oranges and violets, yellows and blues, even pinks and yellows and you will add a vibrant dimension to your flower arranging.

Above: These bright yellow daffodils are complemented by the dark pieces of dried bark.

Left: The natural greens, yellows and mauves of these herbs blend perfectly together.

CONTAINERS

. . .

While an enormous range of suitable, practical, purpose-made containers is available to the flower arranger, with a little imagination alternatives will present themselves, often in the form of objects we might not have at first glance expected. An old jug or teapot, a pretty mug that has lost its handle, an unusual-looking tin, a bucket, a jam jar, all these offer the arranger interesting opportunities.

Remember, if the container is for fresh flowers, it must be watertight or properly lined. Consider the scale and proportion of the container both to the particular flowers you are going to use, and the type of arrangement.

Do not forget the container can be a hidden part of the design, simply there to hold the arrangement, or it can be an integral and important feature in the overall arrangement.

BAKING TINS (PANS)

Apart from the usual round, square or rectangular baking tins (pans), a number of novelty shapes are available. Star, heart, club, spade and diamond shaped baking tins (pans) are used to make cakes that are out of the ordinary and they can also be used very effectively to produce interesting flower arrangements.

These tins (pans) are particularly good for massed designs, either of fresh or dried flowers, but remember, the tin may need lining if it is being used for fresh flowers.

BASKETS

Baskets made from natural materials are an obvious choice for country-style, informal displays. However, there is a wide range of basket designs available to suit many different styles.

Large baskets are good for table or static displays while smaller baskets

A simple gold pot perfectly complements this Christmas display of gilded figs.

with handles can be carried by bridesmaids or filled with flowers or plants and made into lovely gifts. Traditional wicker baskets can be obtained which incorporate herbs or lavender in their weave.

Wire or metal baskets offer an ornate alternative to wicker and twig, since the wire can be formed into intricate shapes and also can have a more modern look.

CAST-IRON URNS

More expensive than many other types of container, the investment in a cast-iron urn is repaid by the splendid classic setting it offers for the display of flowers. Whether the arrangement is large and flowing or contemporary and linear, the visual strength of a classical urn shape will provide the necessary underpinning.

Of course the physical weight of a cast-iron urn is a factor to consider; it is a plus in that it will remain stable with the largest of displays but a minus when it comes to moving it!

ENAMELLED CONTAINERS

The appeal of using an enamelled container probably lies in the bright colours available. Containers in strong primary colours work well with similarly brightly coloured flowers to produce vibrant displays.

GALVANIZED METAL BUCKET AND POT

The obvious practical advantage of galvanized metal containers is that they will not rust. The attractive silvered and polished texture is ideal for contemporary displays in both fresh and dried flowers.

Today lots of shapes and sizes of containers are available with a galvanized finish but even an old-fashioned bucket can be used to good effect in flower arranging.

GLASS VASES

A glass vase is often the first thing that springs to mind for flower arranging. And indeed, there is an enormous range of purpose-made vases available.

The proportions of this design give prominence to the classical urn.

Particularly interesting to the serious flower arranger will be simple clear glass vases which are made in all the sizes and geometric shapes you could ever need. Their value lies in their lack of embellishment which allows the arrangement to speak for itself. Remember the clear glass requires that the water be changed regularly and kept scrupulously clean, since below the water is also part of the display.

There are also many other forms of vase – frosted, coloured, textured, and cut glass – and all have their place in the flower arranger's armoury.

PITCHERS

Pitchers of all types are ideal flower receptacles. Ceramic, glass, enamelled or galvanized metal; short, tall, thin, fat – whatever their shape, size or colour, they offer the flower arranger a wide range of options.

Displays can range from the rustic and informal to the grand and extravagant, depending on your choice of pitcher and materials.

A varied selection from the vast range of containers that can by used for flower arranging.

PRE-FORMED PLASTIC FOAM SHAPES

Clean to handle, convenient to use, pre-formed plastic foam comes in a wide range of shapes and sizes such as circles, crosses, rectangles and even "novelty" designs like stars, numerals, hearts and teddy bears. Each shape is a moisture-retaining foam with a watertight backing. Equivalent foam shapes are available for dried flowers.

Although often associated with funeral and sympathy designs, pre-formed plastic foam shapes also offer the flower arranger a variety of bases for many other types of display.

TERRACOTTA PLANT POTS

Traditional or modern, the terracotta pot can be utilized to hold an arrangement of flowers and not just plants. If the arrangement is built in plastic foam, line the pot with cellophane (plastic wrap) before

inserting the foam, to prevent leakage. Alternatively just pop a jam jar or bowl into the pot to hold the water.

The appearance of terracotta pots can be changed very effectively by techniques such as rubbing them with different coloured chalks, or treating them with gold leaf. They can also be aged by the application of organic materials such as sour milk which, if left, will enable a surface growth to develop.

WOODEN TRUGS AND BOXES

Old-fashioned wooden trugs and seedboxes can make charming and effective containers for floral displays. Their rustic appeal makes them particularly suitable for informal country-style designs where the container is an enhancing feature. Rubbing the surface of a wooden container with coloured chalk can create an entirely new look.

Of course you must remember to line the box with waterproof material if fresh flowers or plants are going to be used in the display.

EQUIPMENT

· · ·

The flower arranger can get by with the minimum of equipment when he or she is just starting out. However, as he or she becomes more adventurous, a selection of specialized tools and equipment will be useful. This section itemizes those pieces of equipment used in the projects contained in the book.

CELLOPHANE (PLASTIC WRAP)

As wrapping for a bouquet, cellophane (plastic wrap) can transform a bunch of flowers into a lovely gift, and it has a more practical use as a waterproof lining for containers. Also, it can look very effective scrunched up in a vase of water to support flower stems.

FLORIST'S ADHESIVE

This very sticky glue is supplied in a pot and is the forerunner to the hot, melted adhesive of the glue gun. It is necessary when attaching synthetic ribbons or other materials which might be adversely affected by the heat of a glue gun.

FLORIST'S ADHESIVE TAPE

This is a strong adhesive tape used to secure plastic foam in containers. Although it will stick under most circumstances, avoid getting it too wet as this will limit its adhesive capability.

PLASTIC FOAM

Plastic foam comes in a vast range of shapes, sizes and densities, and is available for both dry and fresh flowers. While the rectangular brick is the most familiar, other shapes are available for specific purposes.

Plastic foam is lightweight, convenient to handle and very easy to cut and shape with just a knife. A brick of plastic foam for fresh flowers soaks up water very quickly

Before starting to build a design make sure you have all the materials close to hand.

(approximately 1½ minutes) but must not be resoaked as the structure alters and its effectiveness will be reduced. Plastic foam for dried flowers can seem too hard for the delicate stems of some flowers but a softer version is available, so consider which type you need before starting the design.

FLORIST'S SCISSORS

A strong, sharp pair of scissors are the flower arranger's most important tool. As well as cutting all those things you would expect, the scissors must also be sturdy enough to cut woody stems and even wires.

FLORIST'S TAPE (STEM-WRAP TAPE)

This tape is not adhesive, but the heat of your hands will help secure it to itself as it is wrapped around a stem

The tape is used to conceal wires and seal stem ends. It is made either from plastic or crêpe paper and it will stretch to provide a thin covering. The tape is available in a range of colours although green is normally used on fresh flowers.

FLORIST'S WIRE

Wire is used to support, control and secure materials, also to extend stems and to replace them where weight reduction is required. The wire tends

to be sold in different lengths. Most of the projects in this book use 36 cm (14 in) lengths. Always use the lightest gauge of wire you can while still providing sufficient support. The most popular gauges are:

1.25mm (18g)	0.28mm (31g)
0.90mm (20g)	0.24mm (32g)
0.71mm (22g)	Silver reel
0.56mm (24g)	*(rose) wires:*
0.46mm (26g)	0.56mm (24g)
0.38mm (28g)	0.32mm (30g)
0.32mm (30g)	0.28mm (32g)

Make sure that the wires are kept in a dry place because any moisture will cause them to rust.

GLOVES

While some flower arranging processes would be impeded by gloves, it makes sense to protect your hands whenever necessary, especially if handling materials with sharp thorns or sap which might irritate the skin. So keep some domestic rubber gloves and heavy-duty gardening gloves in your florist's workbox.

GLUE GUN

The glue gun is an electrically powered device fed by sticks of glue, which it melts to enable the user to apply glue via a trigger action. In floristry it is a relatively recent development but invaluable in allowing the arranger to attach dried or fresh materials to swags, garlands or circlets securely, cleanly and efficiently.

The glue and the tip of the gun are extremely hot, so take care at all times when using a glue gun. Never leave a hot glue gun unattended.

PAPER RIBBON

Paper ribbon is an alternative to satin and synthetic ribbon and is available in a large range of mostly muted, soft

colours. It is sold twisted and rolled up. Cut the length of ribbon required in its twisted state and carefully untwist and flatten it to its full width before creating your bow.

PINHOLDER
The pinholder is a heavy metal disc approximately 2 cm (¾ in) thick which has an even covering of sharp metal pins, approximately 3 cm (1¼ in) long. Pinholders are available in a range of diameter sizes for different displays.

The pinholder is placed under the water and the bottom of the flower stems are pushed on to the pins. The weight of the stems is balanced by the weight of the pinholder. It is ideal for creating *Ikebana*-style displays or twiggy linear arrangements.

RAFFIA
A natural alternative to string and ribbon, raffia has several uses for the flower arranger. It can be used, a few strands at a time, to tie together a hand-arranged, spiralled bunch, or to attach bunches of dried or fresh

Start with the basic equipment and add items as your skill develops.

flowers to garlands and swags. In thicker swathes it can also be used to finish bouquets and arrangements by tying them off and being formed into decorative bows.

ROSE STRIPPER
This ingenious little device is a must when handling very thorny roses. Squeeze the metal claws together and pull the stripper along the stem, and the thorns and leaves will be removed. There is also a blade attachment to cut stem ends at an angle. Always wear thick gardening gloves.

SATIN RIBBON
Available in a large variety of widths and colours, satin ribbon is invaluable to the flower arranger when a celebratory final touch is required.

Satin ribbon is preferable to synthetic ribbon because it looks and feels so much softer. Its only drawback is that it frays when cut.

SECATEURS (GARDEN CLIPPERS)
These are necessary to cut the tougher, thicker stems and branches of foliage. Always handle scissors and secateurs with care and do not leave within the reach of young children.

TWINE
String or twine is essential when tying spiralled bunches, making garlands or attaching foliage to gates and posts.

WIRE MESH
Although plastic foam now offers much more flexibility for the flower arranger, wire mesh still has its place in the florist's armoury.

When creating large displays, wire mesh is essential to strengthen the plastic foam and prevent it from crumbling when large numbers of stems are pushed into it. The mesh should be cut in lengths from the roll, crumpled slightly, laid over the top and wrapped around the sides of the foam and wedged between it and the container, then secured in place with florist's adhesive tape.

TECHNIQUES

· · ·

TAPING

Stems and wires are covered with florist's tape (stem-wrap tape) for three reasons: first, cut materials which have been wired can no longer take up water and covering with tape seals in the moisture that already exists in the plant; second, the tape conceals the wires, which are essentially utilitarian, and gives a more natural appearance to the false stem; third, wired dried materials are covered with florist's tape (stem-wrap tape) to ensure that the material does not slip out of the wired mount.

1 Hold the wired stem near its top with the end of a length of florist's tape (stem-wrap tape) between the thumb and index finger of one hand. With your free hand, hold the remainder of the length of tape at 45° to the wired stem, keeping it taut. Starting at the top of the stem, just above the wires, rotate the flower slowly to wrap the tape around both the stem and wires, working down. By keeping it taut, the tape will stretch into a thin layer around the stem and wires. Each layer should overlap and stick to the one before. If so desired, you may add flowerheads at different heights as you tape to create units. Finally, fasten off just above the end of the wires by squeezing the tape against itself to stick it securely.

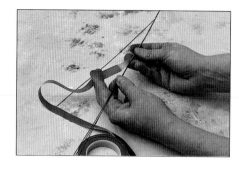

MAKING A STAY WIRE

1 Group together four .71 wires, each overlapping the next by about 3 cm (1¼ in). Start taping the wires together from one end using florist's tape (stem-wrap tape). As the tape reaches the end of the first wire add another .71 wire to the remaining three ends of wire and continue taping, and so on, adding wires and taping four together until you achieve the required length of stay wire.

SINGLE LEG MOUNT

This is for wiring flowers which have a strong natural stem or where a double weight of wire is not necessary to support the material.

1 Hold the flowers or foliage between the thumb and index finger of one hand while taking the weight of the material (i.e. the flowerheads) cross the top of your hand. Position a wire of the appropriate weight and length behind

the stem about one-third up from the bottom. Bend the wire ends together with one leg shorter than the other. Holding the short wire leg parallel with the stem, wrap the long wire leg firmly around both the stem and the other wire leg three or four times. Straighten the long wire leg to extend the stem. Cover the stem and wire with florist's tape (stem-wrap tape).

DOUBLE LEG MOUNT

This is formed in the same way as the single leg mount but extends the stem with two equal length wire legs.

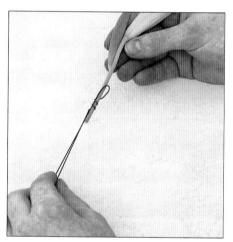

1 Hold the flower or foliage between the thumb and index finger of one hand while taking the weight of the plant material (i.e. the flowerheads) across the top of your hand. Position a wire of appropriate weight and length behind the stem about one-third of the way up from the bottom. One-third of the wire should be to one side of the stem with two-thirds to the other. Bend the wire parallel to the stem. One leg should now be about twice as long as the other.

Holding the shorter leg against the stem, wrap the longer leg around both stem and the other wire to secure. Straighten both legs which should now be of equal length.

PIPPING

Pipping is the process whereby small flowerheads are removed from a main stem to be wired individually. This process can be used for intricate work with small delicate plant materials.

1 Bend a thin silver wire into a hairpin about its centre and twist at the bend to form a small loop above the two projecting legs.

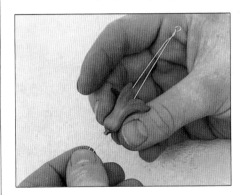

2 Push the legs into the flower centre, down through its throat, and out of its base to create a stem.

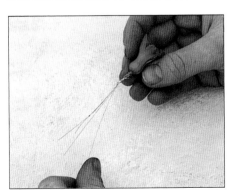

3 Using more silver wire, double leg mount this stem with any natural existing stem, and tape if required.

UNITS

A unit is the composite stem formed from two or more pieces of plant material. Units of small flowers can be used in corsages and hair-comb decorations, and units of larger flowers in wired wedding bouquets.

Units should be made up of one type of material only. For small units, first wire and tape the individual flowerheads, buds or leaves.

1 Start with the smallest of the plant material and attach a slightly larger head to it by taping the wires together. Position the larger head in line with the bottom of the first item. Increase the size of the items as you work downward.

For units of larger flowers you may have to join the wire stems by double leg mounting them with an appropriate weight of wire before taping.

EXTENDING THE LENGTH OF A STEM

Flowerheads with short stems, and flowers that are delicate may need the extra support of an extended stem. There are two methods of extending a stem.

1 Wire the flowerhead using the appropriate method and correct

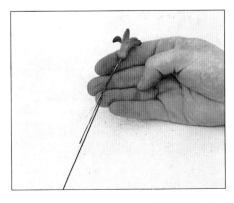

weight of wire. Then single leg mount the wired flowerhead using a .71 wire and tape the wires and any natural stem with florist's tape (stem-wrap tape).

Alternatively, push a .71 wire into the base of the flowerhead from the bottom, then at right angles to this push through a .38 silver wire from one side to the other.

Bend the .38 silver wire so that the two ends point downwards, parallel to the .71 wire. Wrap one leg of .38 wire firmly around its other leg and the .71 wire. Cover with florist's tape (stem-wrap tape).

WIRING AN OPEN FLOWERHEAD

This is a technique for the wiring of individual heads of lily, amaryllis and tulip and is also suitable for small, soft or hollow-stemmed flowers such as anemones and ranunculus.

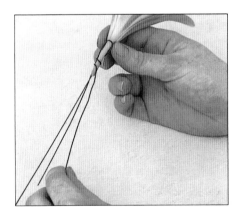

1 Cut the stem of the flower to around 4 cm (1½ in). Push one .71 wire up through the inside of the stem and into the base of the flowerhead. Double leg mount the stem and its internal wire with a .71 wire. Tape the stem and wire.

The internal wire will add strength to the flower's natural stem and the double leg mount will ensure that the weight of the flowerhead is given sufficient support.

WIRING A ROSE HEAD

Roses have relatively thick, woody stems so to make them suitable for use in intricate work, such as buttonholes, headdresses and corsages, the natural stem will need to be replaced with a wire stem.

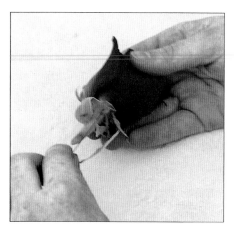

Cut the stem of the rose to a length of approximately 3 cm (1¼ in).

Push one end of a .71 wire through the seed box of the rose at the side. Holding the head of the rose carefully in one hand (as it is very fragile), wrap the wire several times firmly around and down the stem. Straighten the remaining wire to extend the natural stem. Cover the wire and stem with florist's tape (stem-wrap tape).

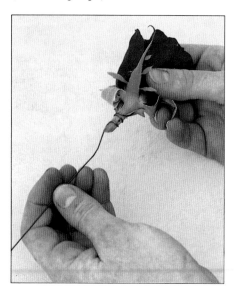

WIRING FRUIT AND VEGETABLES

Using fruit and vegetables in swags, wreaths and garlands, or securing them in plastic foam displays will require wiring them first. The method will depend on the item to be wired and how it is to be used.

Heavy fruits and vegetables, such as oranges, lemons or bulbs of garlic, will need a heavy .71 wire or even .90. The wire should be pushed through the item, just above its base from one side to the other. Push another wire through the item at right angles to the first and bend all four projecting wires to point downwards.

1 Depending on how the fruit or vegetables will be used, either cut the wires to a suitable length to be pushed into plastic foam, or twist the wires together to form a single stem.

2 Small delicate fruits and vegetables such as mushrooms or figs need careful handling as their flesh is easily damaged. They normally only need one wire. Push the wire through the

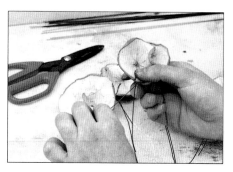

Preserved (dried) apple slices require careful handling when wiring.

base of the item from one side to the other and bend the two projecting wires downwards. Depending on how the material is to be used, either twist to form a single stem, or trim to push into plastic foam.

For the soft materials .71 is the heaviest weight of wire you will require. In some instances, fruit or vegetables can be attached or secured in an arrangement by pushing a long wire "hairpin" right through the item and into the plastic foam behind.

3 Fruit or vegetables that have a stem, such as bunches of grapes or artichokes, can be double leg mounted on their stems with appropriate weight wires.

Extend the length of a starfish by double leg mounting one of its legs.

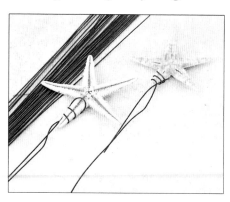

FRUIT AND VEGETABLES IN FLOWER DISPLAYS

The colours and textures of fruit and vegetables can provide harmony or contrast to enhance flower arrangements. The acid colours of citrus fruits, and autumn tints of apples and pears are all readily available to the flower arranger.

Some fruits such as pomegranates, passion fruits and blood oranges are particularly attractive when they have

The strong forms of fruit and vegetables lend themselves well to displays such as this wall swag (above) and unusual obelisk (right). Careful wiring ensures the materials stay in position.

been cut or torn open to reveal their flesh. However, remember that open fruits will deteriorate quickly so only use them for short-term displays at special events, parties or dinners.

Vegetables might seem a surprising choice for use in flower arrangements but the subtle colours and textures can be combined with blooms to beautiful effect. Purple artichokes, almost black aubergines (eggplants), pink and white garlic bulbs, and bright red radishes can give depth, substance and a focal point to a variety of differnt arrangements.

Dried citrus fruit slices look wonderful, and will retain a slight tangy perfume.

COVERING A WIRE HANDLE WITH RIBBON

To make carrying a wired bouquet more comfortable the wired stems can be made into a handle.

1 To ensure that the handle is the correct length, trim it to about 1.5 cm (½ in) longer than the diagonal measurement across your palm. Cover the wire handle with florist's stem-wrap tape. Hold the bouquet in one hand, and with your thumb, trap a long length of 2.5 cm (1 in) wide ribbon against the binding point of the bouquet, leaving approximately a 10 cm (4 in) length of ribbon above your thumb.

Take the long end of the ribbon down the handle, under its end and approximately half way up the other side. Hold it in place there with the little finger of your hand, making sure that your thumb remains firmly in place at the binding point.

2 Wind the ribbon back over itself, around and down the handle to its end. Next wind the ribbon back up the handle all the way to the binding point, covering the ribbon already in place and the tape on the handle.

3 Take the winding end of the ribbon, and the excess 10 cm (4 in) at the other end, and tie in a knot at the binding point. Finish in a bow and trim the ribbon ends.

LINING A CONTAINER

If a container is to be used for arranging fresh flowers then clearly it must be watertight. However, if you are arranging your flowers in plastic foam then you can use a container which is not watertight provided you line it with polythene or cellophane (plastic wrap).

Cut a piece of cellophane (plastic wrap) slightly larger than the container and push it into the container making sure that it gets into all the corners and has no holes or tears. Cut the soaked plastic foam with a knife to fit the container and wedge it in. Trim the lining around the edge of the container and secure the plastic foam in place with florist's adhesive tape.

Be sure not to allow any water to get between the lining and the container and do not trim the lining too short as the water may spill over the top and down on to the sides.

SPIRALLING STEMS

A hand-tied spiralled bouquet is an excellent way of presenting flowers as a gift because they are already arranged and the recipient only has to cut the string and place the flowers in a suitable vase.

1 Place all the materials close to hand so that you can pick up individual stems easily. Hold a strong stem of foliage or flowers in one hand approximately two-thirds down from its top. Build the bouquet by adding one stem of your materials at a time, gradually turning the bunch in your hand as you do so to produce a spiral of stems. If you add your materials in a pre-planned repeating sequence, it will ensure an even distribution of different varieties throughout the bouquet. By occasionally varying the position you hold the stems as you add them it is possible to create a domed shape to the bunch.

2 When you have completed the bunch tie securely with twine, raffia or ribbon around the point where all the stems cross – the binding point.

3 Trim the stem ends so they are even, remembering that the stems below the binding point should comprise about one-third of the overall height of the finished bouquet.

STITCHING LEAVES

Stitching is a technique for wiring a leaf in such a way that it can be held in a "naturally" bent position.

1 Hold a leaf in one hand with its back facing you and very carefully stitch a thin wire horizontally through the central vein and back out again. You may need to practise this at first.

Bend the legs of the wire down along the stem forming a hairpin shape. Hold one leg of wire against the stem of the leaf and wrap the other leg of wire around both stem and wire several times. Then straighten the legs and tape with florist's tape (stem-wrap tape).

Below: Very fine reel wire can also be used to secure material to basket edgings.

MATERIALS

. . .

half block plastic foam

. . .

*2 small terracotta pots,
1 slightly larger than the other*

. . .

cellophane (plastic wrap)

. . .

knife

. . .

scissors

. . .

ming fern

. . .

ivy leaves

. . .

*5 stems 'Santini' spray
chrysanthemums*

. . .

6 stems purple phlox

. . .

18 dark red roses

*Very quick and easy to make,
the simplicity of these charming
decorations is irresistible.*

FRESH VALENTINE
TERRACOTTA POTS
. . .

With luck, Valentine's Day brings with it red roses, but these small jewel-like arrangements present them in an altogether different way. The deep red of the roses visually·links the two pots: contrasting with the acid lime green of 'Santini' chrysanthemums in one, and combining richly with purple phlox in the other.

1 Soak the plastic foam in water. Line both terracotta pots with cellophane (plastic wrap). Cut the foam into small blocks and wedge into the lined pots. Trim the cellophane to fit. Do not trim too close to the edge of the pot.

2 Build a dome-shaped foliage outline in proportion to each pot. In the larger pot, push the stems of ming fern into the plastic foam and in the small pot push the ivy leaves into the foam.

3 In the larger pot, arrange 'Santini' chrysanthemums amongst the ming fern. In the small pot, distribute the phlox amongst the ivy to emphasize the dome shapes of both.

4 Strip the leaves from the dark red roses, cut the stems to the desired lengths and arrange evenly throughout both displays.

SMALL FRESH ROSE VALENTINE'S RING

· · ·

While this delightful floral circlet could be used at any time of the year, the impact created by the massed red roses makes it particularly appropriate to Valentine's Day. It can be hung on a wall or, with a candle at its centre, used as a table decoration for a romantic dinner for two.

MATERIALS
· · ·
*plastic foam ring, 15 cm
(6 in) diameter*
· · ·
dark green ivy leaves
· · ·
.71 wires
· · ·
bun moss
· · ·
20 dark red roses
· · ·
scissors

If you receive a Valentine's Day bouquet of red roses, why not recycle them? After the rose blooms have fully blown open, cut down their stems for use in this circlet to extent their lives. Finally dehydrate the circlet and continue to use it as a dried flower display.

1 Soak the plastic foam ring in water. Push individual, medium-sized ivy leaves into the foam to create an even foliage outline all around the ring.

2 Make hairpin shapes out of the .71 wires and pin small pieces of bun moss on to the foam ring between the ivy leaves. Do this throughout the foliage but to a thinner density than the ivy.

3 Cut the rose stems to approximately 3.5 cm (1½ in) long and push them into the foam until the ring is evenly covered. The ivy leaves should still be visible in-between the rose heads.

DRIED VALENTINE
DECORATION IN A BOX
· · ·

MATERIALS
· · ·
*1 block plastic foam
(for dried flowers)*
· · ·
knife
· · ·
heart-shaped box
· · ·
scissors
· · ·
1 bunch dried red roses
· · ·
2 bunches dried lavender
· · ·
*2 bunches dried poppy seed
heads*
· · ·
1 bunch Nigella orientalis

*This arrangement is easy to
make, but to get the best effect
you must not scrimp on
materials. The flowerheads
need to be massed together very
tightly to hide the foam.*

This display, in a heart-shaped box, demonstrates that dried flowers and seed heads look very striking and attractive when massed in groups of one type. Filled with romantic roses and scented lavender, this display can be made as a gift for Valentine's Day or simply as a treat for yourself. It can also be made at any other time of year using a different-shaped box.

1 Stand the block of plastic foam on its end and carefully slice in half down its length with a knife. Then shape both pieces, using the box as a template, so that they will each fit into one half of the box. Fit these two halves into the heart-shaped box ensuring that they fit snugly.

2 Divide the heart shape into quarters, separating each section by a line of the materials to be used. Fill one quarter with rose heads, one with lavender, one with poppy seed heads and the last with *Nigella orientalis*. Make sure that all the material heads are at the same level.

Valentine's Heart Circlet

Instead of the traditional dozen red roses, why not give the love of your life a wall hanging decoration for Valentine's Day?

Set your heart (in this case wooden) in a circlet of dried materials full of romantic associations — red roses to demonstrate your passion, honesty to affirm the truth of your feelings and lavender as sweet as your love.

MATERIALS
· · ·
33 dried red rose heads
· · ·
scissors
· · ·
.38 silver wire
· · ·
florist's tape (stem-wrap tape)
· · ·
55 stems dried lavender
· · ·
10 stems dried honesty
· · ·
.71 wires
· · ·
1 small wooden heart, on a string

This takes a little more effort than ordering a bunch of flowers from your florist, but that effort will be seen as a measure of your devotion.

1 Cut the dried rose stems to approximately 2.5 cm (1 in) and individually double leg mount on .38 silver wires, then cover the stems with tape. Group three rose heads together and double leg mount on .38 wire, then cover the stems with tape. Repeat the process for all the rose heads, making in total eleven groups.

Group the dried lavender into bunches of five stems and double leg mount on .38 silver wire, then tape. Repeat the process for all the lavender stems, making in total eleven groups.

Cut individual pods from the stems of dried honesty and group into threes, double leg mounting them together on .38 silver wires and taping. Make eleven groups in total.

Make a stay wire from .71 wires.

2 Lay a group of the honesty pods over one end of the stay wire and tape on securely. Then add, so that they just overlap, a group of lavender stems followed by a group of rose heads, taping each group to the stay wire. Keep repeating this sequence, all the while bending the stay wire into a circle.

3 When the circle is complete, cut off any excess stay wire leaving approximately 3 cm (1¼ in) to overlap. Then tape the two ends together through the dried flowers to secure. Tie the string from the wooden heart on to the stay wire between the dried blooms, so that the heart hangs in the centre of the circlet.

CHILDREN'S PARTY PIECES

· · ·

MATERIALS

· · ·

1 block plastic foam

· · ·

knife

· · ·

3 enamel mugs

· · ·

scissors

· · ·

*24 pink and yellow
"mini-gerbera"*

*The gerbera's sugary colouring
means the display can be
integrated with the contents of
the table – surround them with
jelly and blancmange or have
them emerging from a
mountain of sweets!*

Most people probably think that flowers are wasted on a children's party, but if we can make them fun, then why not?

Gerbera are extraordinary in their simple form and bright colours, and look like a child's idea of a flower. In this display the gerbera are arranged upright and apparently unsupported in simple containers, just like a child's drawing.

1 Soak the block of plastic foam in water. Using a knife, cut small pieces of foam and wedge them into the bottom of each mug so that they take up about one third of the depth.

2 Cut the gerbera stems so that they are approximately 5 cm (2 in) taller than the mug. Push the stem ends into the foam, keeping the flowers upright and pushing some in further than others to get slight variations of height.

SIMPLE EASTER DISPLAY

. . .

This display strips away all embellishments and relies entirely on the intrinsic beauty of the flowers themselves for its impact. To heighten the impact, the flowers are massed in one type only in each container.

The displays are appropriate to Easter because they use familiar flowers which are associated with spring and convey the message of rebirth.

MATERIALS
. . .
50 stems pale blue grape hyacinth
. . .
1 tea-cup
. . .
scissors
. . .
4 pale pink 'Angelique' tulips
. . .
2 pitchers (1 larger than the other)
. . .
15 mauve crocus flowers
. . .
30 stems of narcissi (some cream, some white)
. . .
2 jam jars

1 Measure the grape hyacinth against the tea-cup and cut their stems so that only the heads can be seen above the rim. Also cut the 'Angelique' tulip stems so that only the heads project above the rim of the smaller pitcher. Again, cut the crocus stems so that only their flowerheads are visible above the rim of the larger pitcher. Four tulip heads is sufficient for this small display.

2 Trim the narcissi stems so that the overall height of the flowers is twice the height of the jar. Loosely arrange a mixture of both varieties in each jar. By using a variety of containers the finished display has a good variation of height.

The displays can be grouped together or used individually around the house. They are simple to make, but remember simplicity is often the essence of good design!

EASTER WREATH

$\cdot \ \cdot \ \cdot$

MATERIALS

· · ·

*plastic foam ring,
30 cm (12 in) diameter*

· · ·

elaeagnus foliage

· · ·

scissors

· · ·

5 polyanthus plants

· · ·

8 pieces of bark

· · ·

.71 wires

· · ·

3 blown eggs

· · ·

2 enamel spoons

· · ·

70 stems daffodils

· · ·

raffia

*Whether in the church or
home, this delightful Easter
decoration will bring pleasure
to all who view it.*

Easter is a time of hope and regeneration and this bright Easter wreath visually captures these feelings. It overflows with the floral symbols of spring with daffodils and polyanthus, and contains eggs, a symbol of birth.

The vibrant colours and the flowers, arranged to look as though they are still growing, give the wreath a fresh, natural glow. There is also a touch of humour in the crossed enamel spoons.

1 Soak the foam ring in water and arrange an even covering of elaeagnus stems, approximately 7.5 cm (3 in) long, in the foam. At five equidistant positions, add groups of three polyanthus leaves.

3 Arrange the polyanthus flowers in single-coloured groups as though they are growing by pushing their stems into the plastic foam. Be sure to leave a section of the ring clear for the eggs and spoons. Cut the daffodils to a stem length of approximately 7.5 cm (3 in) and between four groups of polyanthus arrange groups of 15 daffodils, pushing their stems into the plastic foam.

2 Wire the eight pieces of bark by bending a .71 wire around the middle and twisting to achieve a tight grip. Position the pieces of bark equidistant around the ring by pushing the protruding wires into the plastic foam.

4 Bend .71 wires around the spoons and twist. In the gap left on the ring position one of the spoons, wrapping the wire ends around to the back of the ring. Twist the wires together tightly so that the spoon is embedded in the foam. Do this with both spoons, arranged so that they cross. Wrap raffia around the eggs, crossing it over underneath and tying it on the side. Bend .71 wires around the eggs, twisting the ends together gently. Arrange the remaining daffodils and polyanthus flowers around the eggs and spoons.

RUBY WEDDING
DISPLAY

• • •

Designed as a table arrangement complete with celebratory bow around its container, this display of rich and passionate colours would be a magnificent gift.

Formal looking, but simple in its construction, this Ruby Wedding arrangement is a lavish mass of deep purple tulips and velvet red roses set against the dark glossy green of camellia leaves. A beautiful paper bow completes the effect.

1 Approximately three-quarters fill the bowl with water. Cut the stems of camellia and roses to 7.5 cm (3 in) longer than the depth of the container. Arrange the camellia stems in the bowl to create a low domed foliage outline within which the flowers will be arranged. Arrange half the roses evenly throughout the camellia.

2 Cut the tulip stems to approximately 7cm (3 in) longer than the depth of the bowl and strip away any remaining lower leaves from the stems. Position the tulips in the display, distributing them evenly throughout the roses and camellia. Finally add the remaining roses evenly throughout the arrangement to complete a dense, massed flower effect of deep red hues.

3 Form a festive bow from the paper ribbon. The bow should be substantial but it is important that it is kept in scale with the display. To complete the arrangement tie the bow to the container so that it sits on the front.

BABY BIRTH GIFT

· · ·

*The choice of soft subtle
colours means it is suitable for
either boy or girl. There is also
the added bonus of the
beautiful scents of the phlox
and dried lavender.
Since the arrangement has its
own container it is particularly
convenient for a recipient in
hospital, avoiding, as it does,
the need to find a vase!
Finally, the container can be
kept and used after the life of
the display.*

Celebrate a baby's birth by giving the parents this very pretty arrangement in an unusual but practical container. The display incorporates double tulips, ranunculus, phlox and spray roses, with small leaves of *Pittosporum*. It is the delicacy of the flowers and foliage which make it appropriate for a baby.

1 Soak the plastic foam in water, cut it to fit the small metal bucket and wedge it firmly in place. Cut the *Pittosporum* to a length of 12 cm (4¾ in) and clean the leaves from the lower part of the stems. Push the stems into the plastic foam to create an overall domed foliage outline within which the flowers can be arranged.

2 Cut the 'Angelique' tulips to a stem length of 10 cm (4 in) and distribute them evenly throughout the foliage. Cut individual off-shoots from the main stems of the spray roses to a length of 10 cm (4 in), and arrange throughout the display, with full blooms at the centre and buds around the outside.

3 Cut the ranunculus and phlox to a stem length of 10 cm (4 in) and distribute both throughout the display. Cut the lavender to a stem length of 12 cm (4¾ in) and arrange in groups of three stems evenly throughout the flowers and foliage. Tie the ribbon around the bucket and finish in a generous bow.

PLANTED BASKET FOR BABY
. . .

This display of pot plants in a basket makes a lovely gift to celebrate the birth of a baby. It is easy to make and quick to prepare, and is a long-lasting alternative to a cut flower arrangement.

MATERIALS
. . .
1 wire basket
. . .
2 handfuls Spanish moss
. . .
cellophane (plastic wrap)
. . .
scissors
. . .
*3 pots miniature white
cyclamen*
. . .
3 pots lily-of-the-valley
. . .
paper ribbon

The combination of two simple and delicate white plants, baby cyclamen and lily-of-the-valley, gives the design charm and purity, indeed everything about it says "baby".

1 Line the wire basket with generous handfuls of Spanish moss, then carefully line the moss with cellophane (plastic wrap). Trim the cellophane to fit around the rim of the basket.

2 Remove the plants from their pots carefully. Loosen the soil and the roots a little before planting them in the basket, alternating the cyclamen with the lily-of-the-valley.

3 Make sure that the plants are firmly bedded in the basket. Make two small bows from the paper ribbon and attach one to each side of the basket at the base of the handle.

DRIED FLOWER HORSESHOE
BABY GIFT
· · ·

MATERIALS
· · ·
14 heads dried, white roses
· · ·
*42 heads dried, bleached
honesty*
· · ·
60 heads dried phalaris grass
· · ·
scissors
· · ·
.38 silver wire
· · ·
florist's tape (stem-wrap tape)
· · ·
.71 wires
· · ·
ribbon

W hat could be nicer for new parents than to receive a floral symbol of good
luck on the birth of their baby?

The whites and pale green of this dried flower horseshoe make it a perfect gift
or decoration for the nursery.

1 Cut the rose stems, honesty stems and
phalaris grass to approximately 2.5 cm
(1 in) long. Double leg mount the roses
individually on .38 silver wire, then tape.
Double leg mount the phalaris heads in
groups of five on .38 silver wire, and the
honesty in clusters of three on .38 silver
wire. Tape each group.

2 Make a stay wire approximately 30 cm
(12 in) long from .71 wire on which
the horseshoe will be built.

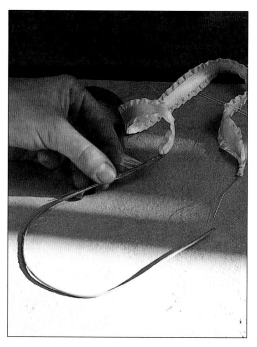

3 Form three small bows approximately
4 cm (1½ in) wide from the ribbon
and bind them at their centres with .38
silver wire. Cut a 30 cm (12 in) length of
ribbon and double leg mount both ends
separately with .38 silver wire. This will
form the handle for the horseshoe.

4 Form the stay wire into a horseshoe
shape. Tape one wired end of the
ribbon to one end of the stay wire. Tape
one of the bows over the junction of the
ribbon and stay wire, making sure it is
securely in place.

5 Starting at the bow, tape the flowers and foliage to the stay wire, to its mid point, in the following repeating sequence: phalaris, rose, honesty. Tape a bow at the centre and tape the last bow and the remaining ribbon end to the other end of the stay wire. Work the flowers in the same sequence back to the centre point.

While making the horseshoe is relatively-time consuming, the effort will no doubt have created something of such sentimental value that it will be kept forever.

GOLDEN WEDDING
BOUQUET
· · ·

*20 stems golden yellow
ranunculus*

· · ·

20 stems mimosa

· · ·

gold twine

· · ·

scissors

· · ·

*2 sheets gold-coloured tissue
paper in 2 shades*

· · ·

*piece gold-coloured fabric
approx. 46 cm (18 in) long,
15 cm (6 in) wide*

· · ·

gold dust powder

*This arrangement makes a
flamboyant gift but nonetheless
is as simple to create as a
hand-tied bouquet. It can be
unwrapped and placed straight
into a vase of water, with no
need for further arranging.*

This shimmering bouquet makes an unequivocal Golden Wedding statement. Unashamed in its use of yellows and golds, the colours are carried right through the design in the flowers, the wrapping paper, the binding twine and the ribbon, even to a fine sprinkling of gold dust powder.

1 Lay out the stems of ranunculus and mimosa so that they are easily accessible. Clean the stems of leaves from about a third of the way down. Holding a stem of ranunculus in your hand, start to build the bouquet by adding alternate stems of mimosa and ranunculus, turning the flowers in your hand all the while so that the stems form a spiral.

2 When all the flowers have been arranged in your hand, tie the stems together at the binding point with the gold twine. When secured, trim the stems to a length approximately one-third of the overall height of the bouquet.

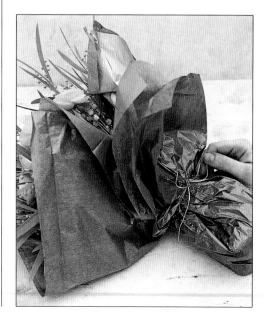

3 To wrap the bouquet, lay the two shades of tissue on top of each other and lay the bouquet diagonally on top. Pull up the sides of the paper, then the front, and hold these in place by tying the gold twine around the binding point. To complete the display, tie the gold fabric around the binding point and create a bow. Scatter a little gold dust powder over the flowers. Separate the sheets of tissue to give a fuller appearance.

CUT FLOWERS AS A GIFT

· · ·

*Because it is a spiral-tied
bouquet it can be placed
straight into a container
without the need for further
arranging.*

This elegant, long-stemmed bouquet is the gift for a very special occasion. This is a cool and uncluttered arrangement in which the cream colours and soft surfaces of calla lilies and French tulips are brought into focus by the coarse textures and irregular shapes of lichen-covered larch twigs. As a finishing touch, the bouquet is wrapped in cellophane (plastic wrap) and tied with raffia in a bow.

1 Set out all materials for easy access. Remove the lower leaves from the tulip stems and cut the larch twigs to a more manageable length.

Start with a calla lily and add twigs and tulips, all the while turning the growing arrangement so that the stems form a spiral.

2 Continue adding stems and larch twigs until all the materials are used. Tie securely at the binding point with raffia. Trim level the stem ends of the completed bouquet, taking care to avoid cutting them too short.

3 Cut a large square of cellophane (plastic wrap) and lay the bouquet diagonally across it. Wrap the cellophane up around the sides of the bouquet to overlap at the front. Tie securely at the binding point and finish with a raffia bow.

FRESH FLOWERS AS A GIFT-WRAP DECORATION

• • •

This is essentially a corsage used to decorate a wrapped gift. It offers the opportunity to make the gift extra special, and to give flowers at the same time. The colour and form of the gerbera and 'Mona Lisa' lily heads are very bold, and this is contrasted with the small delicate bell heads of lily-of-the-valley and lace-like grey lichen on the larch twigs.

1 From the lily stem, cut a 20 cm (7¾ in) length with one bud and one open flower on it. Also cut a single open flower on an 8 cm (3¼ in) stem. Cut six twigs from the larch branch, each about 25 cm (10 in) long. Cut three lily-of-the-valley on stems approximately 15cm (6 in) long, each with a leaf.

Cut one gerbera stem to 18 cm (7 in) long and the second to 14 cm (5½ in) long. Create a flat fan-shaped outline with the lichen-covered larch twigs. Position the longer lily stem in the centre of the fan and the single lily head immediately below.

Next arrange the lily-of-the-valley and gerbera flowerheads around the two open lilies. Tie the stems securely with raffia at the point where they all cross (the binding point).

2 Lay the completed decoration diagonally across the wrapped gift and take a long piece of raffia around it, crossing underneath the parcel and bringing it back up to tie off on top of the stems.

Tie the ribbon around the binding point of the decoration and form it into a bow.

MATERIALS

• • •

1 stem lily 'Mona Lisa'

• • •

scissors

• • •

1 branch lichen-covered larch

• • •

1 small pot lily-of-the-valley

• • •

2 pink gerbera

• • •

raffia

• • •

gift-wrapped present

• • •

ribbon

The decoration is made as a small, tied, flat-based sheaf. This involves no wiring and thus is relatively simple to make, provided you give sufficient thought to the visual balance between the bold and delicate elements.

DRIED FLOWERS AS A GIFT-WRAP DECORATION

· · ·

MATERIALS
· · ·
1 dried sunflower head
· · ·
scissors
· · ·
.71 wires
· · ·
1 small dried pomegranate
· · ·
*3 small pieces dried fungi
(graded in size)*
· · ·
*3 slices dried orange
(graded in size)*
· · ·
.38 silver wires
· · ·
*florist's tape
(stem-wrap tape)*
· · ·
gift-wrapped present
· · ·
raffia

To make a present extra special why not make the wrapping part of the gift? The construction of this display is effectively a dried flower corsage but used to embellish gift wrapping.

It takes a little time to produce but its natural, warm, earthy colours make this a delightful enhancement well worth the effort, and something to keep.

1 Cut the sunflower to a stem length of 2.5 cm (1 in) and double leg mount on a .71 wire. Single leg mount the pomegranates on .71 wire. Double leg mount the small pieces of fungi on .71 wires and the orange slices on .38 silver wires.

2 Wrap all the wired materials with tape, then attach the three orange slices to one side of the sunflower and pomegranate, then attach the three layers of fungi on the other side. Bind all these in place using the .38 silver wire.

3 Trim the wire stems to a length of 5 cm (2 in) and tape together with florist's tape (stem–wrap tape). Tie the raffia around the present and push the wired stem of the decoration under the raffia knot. Secure in place with a .71 wire.

DRIED FLOWERS AS A GIFT
• • •

This is a great way to present dried flowers as a gift. Treat them as you would a tied bunch of cut fresh flowers – make an arranged-in-the-hand, spiral-stemmed bouquet that can be placed straight into a vase.

MATERIALS
• • •
10 small dried pink Protea compacta *buds*
• • •
10 stems dried pink larkspur
• • •
10 stems dried pink peonies
• • •
10 stems dried green amaranthus
• • •
raffia
• • •
scissors
• • •
2 sheets blue tissue paper
• • •
pink ribbon

The deep pink mixture of exotic and garden flowers – protea and amaranthus with peonies and larkspur – makes this a floral gift anyone would be thrilled to receive.

1 Lay out the dried materials so that they are all easily accessible. Start the bouquet with a dried protea held in your hand, add a stem of larkspur, a stem of peony and a stem of amaranthus, all the while turning the growing bunch.

2 Continue until all the dried materials have been used. Tie with raffia at the binding point – where the stems cross each other. Trim the stem ends so that their length is approximately one-third of the overall height of the bouquet.

3 Lay the sheets of tissue paper on a flat surface and place the bouquet diagonally across the tissue. Wrap the tissue paper around the flowers, overlapping it at the front. Tie securely at the binding point with a ribbon and form a bow.

OLD-FASHIONED GARDEN
ROSE TIED BRIDESMAID'S POSY
• • •

Finished with a natural raffia bow, the posy has a fresh, just-gathered look. Happily, it is very simple to make.

This tiny hand-tied posy of blown red and pale apricot roses and mint is designed to accompany the bridesmaid's circlet headdress. The velvet beauty of the contents gives it charm and impact.

1 Remove all thorns and lower leaves from the rose stems. Starting with a rose in one hand, add alternately two stems of mint and one rose stem until all the materials are used. Keep turning the posy as you build to form the stems into a spiral. Finally add the vine leaves to form an edging to the arrangement and tie with twine at the binding point.

2 Trim the ends of the stems so that they are approximately one-third of the overall height of the posy. Tie raffia around the binding point and form it into a secure bow.

CIRCLET HEADDRESS FOR A YOUNG BRIDESMAID

• • •

Although classic in its design, this bridesmaid's circlet headdress is given a contemporary feel by the use of a rich colour combination not usually associated with traditional wedding flowers.

MATERIALS

• • •

*9 individual deep red rose
heads*

• • •

*9 small clusters apricot
spray roses*

• • •

8 small bunches rosehips

• • •

scissors

• • •

.71 stub wires

• • •

9 small individual vine leaves

• • •

.38 silver wires

• • •

9 small bunches mint

• • •

florist's tape (stem-wrap tape)

The small bunches of orange-red rosehips give a substance to the fabric-like texture of the red and apricot coloured roses.

1 Cut all the flowers to a stem length of approximately 2.5 cm (1 in). Wire the individual rose heads with .71 wires. Stitch wire the vine leaves with .38 silver wire. Tape all the wired items.

Make the stay wire with .71 wires approximately 4 cm (1½ in) longer than the circumference of the head. Tape the wired flowers and foliage to the stay wire in the following repeating sequence: individual rose, mint, spray rose, vine leaf, rosehips. As you tape materials to the stay wire, form it into a circle. Leave 4 cm (1½ in) of the stay wire undecorated, overlap it behind the beginning of the circlet and tape securely together through the flowers.

TIED BRIDAL BOUQUET
· · ·

MATERIALS
· · ·

10 stems Lilium
longiflorum
· · ·

10 stems cream-coloured
Eustoma grandiflorum
· · ·

10 stems white
Euphorbia fulgens
· · ·

5 stems Molucella laevis
· · ·

10 stems white aster
'Monte Cassino'
· · ·

10 stems dill
· · ·

10 ivy trails
· · ·

twine
· · ·

scissors
· · ·

raffia

*To create a bouquet of this
size requires quite a large
quantity of materials which
may prove expensive, but the
design lends itself to being
scaled down to suit a tighter
budget by using the same
materials in smaller quantities.*

This classic "shower" wedding bouquet has a generous trailing shape and incorporates *Lilium longiflorum* as its focal flowers, using the traditional, fresh bridal colour combination of white, cream and green.

Because the flowers are left on their stems the bouquet is physically quite heavy; however, visually, the arrangement has a natural, loose appearance with the long, elegant stems of *Euphorbia fulgens* and asters emphasizing the flowing effect.

1 Lay out your materials so that they are easily accessible. Hold one stem of *Lilium longiflorum* in your hand about 25 cm (10 in) down from the top of its flower head. Begin adding the other flowers and ivy trails in a regular sequence to get an even distribution of materials throughout the bouquet. As you do this, keep turning the bunch in your hand to make the stems form a spiral.

2 To one side of the bouquet add materials on longer stems than the central flower – these will form the trailing element of the display. To the opposite side add stems slightly shorter than the central bloom, and this will become the top of the bouquet. Spiralling the stems will enable the short, upper part of the bouquet to come back over the hand when it is being carried. This will ensure a good profile, which is essential to avoid it looking like a shield.

3 When you have finished the bouquet and are satisfied with the shape, tie it with twine at the binding point, firmly, but not too tightly. Cut the stems so that they are 12 cm (4¾ in) long below the binding point. Any shorter and the weight of the bouquet will not be distributed evenly and it will make it difficult to carry.

4 Tie raffia around the binding point and form a bow which sits on top of the stems, facing upward towards the person carrying the bouquet.

SCENTED BRIDESMAID'S BASKET

· · ·

A very young bridesmaid will find it much easier to carry a basket than clutch a posy throughout what must seem an endless wedding ceremony.

This basket uses simple flowers, in a simple colour combination, simply arranged. The result is a beautiful display appropriate for a child.

1 Line the basket with cellophane (plastic wrap) to make it waterproof. Trim the cellophane edges to fit. Soak the quarter block of plastic foam in cold water, trim to fit into the basket and secure in a central position with florist's adhesive tape.

2 Form two small bows from the ribbon. Tie around their centres with .38 silver wires and leave the excess wire projecting at their backs. Bind the handle of the basket with ribbon securing it at either end by tying around with the wire tails of the bows.

3 Build a slightly domed outline throughout the basket with the golden privet, cut to the appropriate length.

4 Cut the tuberose stems to about 9 cm (3½ in) and position in a staggered diagonal across the basket.

5 Cut the freesia stems to approximately 9 cm (3½ in) long and distribute evenly throughout the remainder of the basket. Recess some heads to give greater depth to the finished display.

The wonderful scent of tuberose and freesia is a great bonus to this delightful display.

SCENTED GARLAND
HEADDRESS

· · ·

This garland headdress just oozes the colours and scents of summer: yellows and cream hues mix with the perfumes of tuberose, freesia and mimosa.

The design of the garland allows the headdress simply to sit on the head of the bride or bridesmaid with no need for complex fixing to the hair.

Making the headdress is time consuming and requires a degree of wiring skill, but the result will be well worth the effort. And, of course, it can be kept after the event, although as the flowers are quite fleshy you will need to use the silica gel method of drying.

1 Cut the stems of privet to 5 cm (2 in) and double leg mount with .38 silver wire. Cut the mimosa and crab apple stems to 5 cm (2 in) and, grouping them in separate clusters, double leg mount with .38 silver wire. Wire the freesia and tuberose heads on .38 silver wire using the pipping method, and then double leg mount on .38 silver wire. Tape all the wired materials.

2 With .71 wire make a stay wire approximately 4 cm (1 in) longer than the circumference of the bride's or bridesmaid's head – this extra length will remain undecorated.

3 Tape the materials on to the stay wire in the following sequence: privet, tuberose, mimosa, crab apples and freesia. Curve the stay wire into a circle as you proceed.

4 To finish the headdress neatly, overlap the undecorated end of the stay wire with the decorated beginning. Tape the wires together, through the flowers, to secure.

Yellow Rose Buttonhole
· · ·

The bold choice of vibrant colours characterizes this stunning buttonhole. The yellow roses and elaeagnus, the orange red rosehips and lime green fennel combine to produce a simple, visually strong decoration suitable for either a man or a woman.

MATERIALS
· · ·
scissors
· · ·
1 yellow rose
· · ·
.71 wires
· · ·
5 elaeagnus leaves, graded in size
· · ·
.38 silver wires
· · ·
15 rosehips and leaves
· · ·
1 head fennel
· · ·
florist's tape (stem-wrap tape)
· · ·
.32 silver reel (rose) wire
· · ·
pin

As with all buttonholes, the construction involves wiring which is, of course, time consuming. Make sure you leave plenty of time to create buttonholes on the morning of the ceremony.

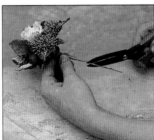

1 Cut the rose stem to 4 cm (1½ in) and wire on .71 wire. Stitch wire all the elaeagnus leaves with .38 silver wires. Group the rosehips, on stems of 4 cm (1½ in), in bunches of five and wire with .38 silver wires. Divide the head of fennel into its component stems and wire in groups with .38 silver wires. Tape all the wired elements.

2 Keeping the rose head central to the display, bind the bunches of fennel and rosehips around it, with .32 silver reel (rose) wire. Bind the elaeagnus leaves to the arrangement with .32 silver reel (rose) wire, placing the largest leaf at the back of the rose, the two smallest at the front, and two medium sized leaves at the side.

3 Trim the wires to approximately 7 cm (2½ in) and tape the wires with florist's tape (stem-wrap tape). Look closely at the completed buttonhole, and, if necessary, bend the leaves down to form a framework for the rose, and adjust the overall shape so that the back of the decoration is flat for pinning to the lapel.

NERINE HAIR COMB

· · ·

*Quite intricate to construct,
this decoration will take
practice before you get it right.*

This beautiful hair decoration, built on a comb, is suitable for the bride who finds a circlet too cumbersome. Delicate in form, but strong in colour, the comb headdress incorporates a variety of textures and colours; bright pink nerines, pink tinged hydrangeas and berries in shades of pink.

1 "Pip" the flowerheads and buds from the main nerine stem. Wire the open nerine florets by passing a bent .38 silver wire with a loop at its end down the throat of the bloom, so that the loop wedges in the narrowest part. Double leg mount each wired flowerhead, the nerine buds and the individual hydrangea florets with .38 silver wires. Cover the stems of all the wired elements with florist's tape (stem-wrap tape).

2 Make two units of nerine with one bud at the top and one slightly open bloom below it. Make two units of two hydrangea florets.

3 Take the two nerine units and bind them together approximately 2 cm (¾ in) below the junction of the stems using the .32 silver reel (rose) wire. Bind the units of hydrangea florets to the nerine units with the .32 wire. Bend both units back to form a straight line, with the nerines slightly longer than the comb and the hydrangea florets slightly shorter.

4 Position an open nerine bloom at the centre of these bound units, with the top of the flower about 5 cm (2 in) above the binding. This is the focal flower. Add the individual flowers and buds to reinforce the shape. Secure them at the binding point with .32 silver reel (rose) wire. Secure the berries at the binding point with .32 silver reel (rose) wire.

Decorative, without being cumbersome, this hair comb makes an eye-catching adornment for a bride's head.

5 When the decoration is complete, separate the wire stems below the binding point into two equal groups and bend them back on themselves parallel to the main stems. Trim the wires at an angle to thin them out, cover each group of wires with tape, to create two prongs.

6 Lay these two wire prongs along the flat back of the comb and tape in position by passing the tape through the teeth in the comb and around the wire prongs. Do this all the way along the length of the comb until the decoration is securely attached.

DRIED FLOWER HAIR COMB

· · ·

MATERIALS

· · ·

scissors

· · ·

*7 dried yellow
rose heads*

· · ·

9 dried phalaris heads

· · ·

.38 silver wires

· · ·

3 small dried starfish

· · ·

9 short stems eucalyptus

· · ·

*5 heads dried, bleached
honesty*

· · ·

*florist's tape
(stem-wrap tape)*

· · ·

plastic hair comb

A decorated hair comb is an alternative headdress to the circlet and is particularly useful if the hair is worn up. This decoration in dried flowers is almost monochromatic, with creamy white roses, silvery-grey eucalyptus, silvery-white honesty and soft green phalaris, with the colourful apricot-coloured dried starfish. The starfish also provide strong graphic shapes, which contrast with the softness of the flowers to create a stunning effect.

1 Cut the rose heads and the phalaris to a stem length of 2 cm (¾ in) and double leg mount them with .38 silver wires. Double leg mount the small starfish with .38 silver wire. Cut two of the eucalyptus stems to a length of 6 cm (2¼ in) and the rest to about 4 cm (1½ in). Double leg mount all the eucalyptus and individual heads of honesty with .38 silver wire. Cover the wired stems of all the materials with florist's tape (stem-wrap tape). Create six units, two containing two roses, two with two phalaris and two with two eucalyptus stems, one at 6 cm (2¼ in) and one at 4 cm (1¼ in), with the longer stem at the top of the unit.

2 Take two eucalyptus units and bind them together about 2 cm (¾ in) below the junction of the stems using .38 silver wire. At the binding point, bend each of two wired units away from each other to form a straight line slightly longer than the length of the comb. Take all the units of rose and phalaris heads and bind them individually to the eucalyptus unit at the binding point and bend each of them flat in the same way. Make all of these units slightly shorter than the eucalyptus.

3 Place an individual rose head at the centre of the bound units with the top about 5 cm (2 in) above the binding point. This will be the focal flower. Position the starfish and the honesty around this central rose head and secure at the binding point with .38 silver wire. Position the individual heads of phalaris and short stems of eucalyptus so that they reinforce the shape and profile of the decoration. Bind all items in place with .38 silver wire.

As well as making an attractive hair decoration, this hair comb can be kept as a momento of a very special day.

4 Next, separate the wire stems below the binding point into two equal groups of wires, bend them apart and back on themselves, parallel to the main stems. Trim the wires at an angle to thin them out before covering each group of wires with tape to create two wired prongs.

5 Lay these two wire prongs along the top of the comb and tape into position by passing the tape between the teeth in the comb and around the wire prongs. Do this all the way along the length of the comb until the decoration is securely attached.

CHURCH PORCH DECORATION

· · ·

MATERIALS

· · ·

gloves

· · ·

secateurs

· · ·

20 bunches long ivy trails

· · ·

twine

· · ·

6 large branches rosehips

· · ·

raffia

· · ·

scissors

This type of decoration is hard work but if you really go for it, the result will be spectacular.

Church festivals, weddings and christenings offer the flower arranger an opportunity to work on a large scale by decorating the church porch. To be successful, the display must have dramatic impact, although it can be simple in its material content.

This porch decoration is designed to look natural, almost as though it is growing out of the structure. Flowers would have been lost in the green mass of ivy, so colour contrast is provided by branches of red rosehips (branches of seasonal blossom would also have the necessary visual strength).

1 Generously drape the ivy trails over the supporting beam of the porch roof starting from the outsides and working towards the centre. As you drape the ivy over the beam, secure at regular intervals with twine.

2 Continue draping the ivy until the beam is evenly covered. Then, again, starting from the outsides, position the branches of rosehips on the top of the ivy trails to hang over the front of the porch.

3 Firmly secure the branches of rosehips in position with twine. Finally form a large bow with the raffia and attach it to the central vertical strut above the rosehips and ivy.

OLD-FASHIONED GARDEN ROSE WEDDING CORSAGE

• • •

MATERIALS

• • •

8 stems rose leaves

• • •

scissors

• • •

3 rose heads graded thus: in bud, just open, fully open

• • •

3 small vine leaves

• • •

.38 silver wires

• • •

florist's tape (stem-wrap tape)

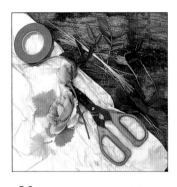

Using just one type of flower with its own foliage and three individual leaves ensures the result is simple yet elegant.

This delicate rose corsage would provide the perfect finishing touch for that special wedding outfit. However, it is best to remember that old-fashioned garden roses are really only available in the summer months.

1 Cut the stems of the rose leaves to length thus: two at 6 cm (2¼ in), two at 4 cm (1½ in), four at 3 cm (1⅛ in). Cut the rose head stems to 4 cm (1½ in) Cut the vine leaf stems to 2.5 cm (1 in) and stitch wire with .38 silver wire.

Make two "units" of rose leaves each with one 6 cm (2¼ in) stem and one 4 cm (1½ in) stem. Make a "unit" using the two smaller rose heads.

Hold one unit of rose leaves in your hand and place the unit of rose heads on top so that the leaves project slightly above the upper rose head. Bind the units together with .38 silver wire, 6 cm (2¼ in) below the lower rose head.

Add the second unit of rose leaves lower and to the left of the first. Add the fully opened rose (the focal flower) with the top of its head level with the bottom of the rose above. Bind to the corsage.

Position the vine leaves around the focal flower and bind in place. Position the remaining individual rose leaves slightly recessed around the focal flower and bind in place.

Trim off the ends of the wires approximately 5 cm (2 in) below the focal flower and cover with tape. Adjust as desired.

WEDDING BASKET

. . .

It has long been a tradition that female guests at weddings are given a "gift" to take home with them. These often take the form of a silk tulle bag containing pastel-coloured sugar almonds.

This symbolically romantic heart-shaped basket is decorated with fresh flowers so that it can be used as a container for such gifts.

MATERIALS

. . .

scissors

. . .

*10 heads white alstromeria
'Ice cream'*

. . .

10 heads white ranunculus

. . .

*10 heads white spray rose
'Princess'*

. . .

*10 clusters small,
white phlox buds
'Rembrandt'*

. . .

.38 silver wires

. . .

1 bunch pittosporum

. . .

florist's tape (stem-wrap tape)

. . .

*1 heart-shaped basket
(loose weave)*

. . .

.32 silver reel (rose) wire

1 Cut all the flowerheads and foliage to a stem length of approximately 2.5 cm (1 in). Double leg mount all the flowers and foliage with one or two .38 silver wires, depending on the weight of each flowerhead. You will need about 25 small, wired stems of pittosporum foliage. Tape all the wired elements with florist's tape (stem-wrap tape). Lay out your materials, ready to decorate the basket one side at a time.

Placed on each table at the wedding reception and filled with sugar almonds, the basket will also make a very attractive decoration in itself.

2 Lay a stem of pittosporum at the basket's centre. Stitch .32 silver reel (rose) wire through the basket and over the pittosporum stem. Stitch a bud of alstromeria over the foliage, followed by a rose head, more pittosporum, a ranunculus head and a cluster of phlox.

3 Repeat this sequence until you reach the bottom point, then stitch .32 silver reel (rose) wire through the basket weave to secure. Decorate the other side of the heart basket, this time working in the opposite direction. Again secure with .32 silver reel (rose) wire.

ORCHID CORSAGE
· · ·

MATERIALS
· · ·

7 orchid flowerheads (spray orchids)

· · ·

.38 silver wires

· · ·

5 small Virginia creeper leaves

· · ·

10 stems of bear grass

· · ·

.71 wire

· · ·

florist's tape (stem-wrap tape)

· · ·

scissors

The corsage is relatively intricate to make, but the effort required is rewarded with a particularly stylish accessory.

Orchids tend to be naturally ostentatious flowers and as such are perfect for wedding corsages. The grandeur of the spray orchids make them particularly suitable for the mothers of the bride and groom.

1 Double leg mount the orchid heads individually with .38 silver wires. Stitch wire the Virginia creeper leaves by passing a .38 silver wire through the leaflets and bending the wire down to form a false stem, double leg mount this and whatever natural stem exists with another .38 silver wire. Taking two stems of bear grass, bend them into a loop with a tail, double leg mount this on a .71 wire. Make a total of five bear-grass loops, then tape all of the wired materials.

2 Hold a wired orchid head between your index finger and thumb, add a wired leaf, then bind these together approximately 4 cm (1 in) down the wired stem using the .38 silver wire. Add the rest of the materials creating a very small wired posy, binding them in place with the .38 silver wire. Make sure that the binding point remains in one place.

3 When positioning the materials ensure that the looped bear grass is evenly distributed and that the leaves are also arranged in a regular way through the design so that it is evenly balanced.

4 When everything is wired in place trim the wire stems to about 5 cm (2 in) and cover with florist's tape (stem-wrap tape). Once completed, you may wish to gently manoeuvre the individual elements to achieve the most satisfactory effect.

This stunning corsage can add an element of glamour to even the simplest of clothing.

YELLOW ROSE
BRIDESMAID'S BASKETS
• • •

FOR EACH BASKET YOU
WILL NEED:

half block plastic foam

· · ·

knife

· · ·

1 small basket (plastic lined)

· · ·

scissors

· · ·

30 stems birch,
approximately 10 cm
(4 in) long

· · ·

10 stems yellow roses

· · ·

5 stems fennel

· · ·

raffia

The flowers are secured in
plastic foam and will stay fresh
for the bridesmaid to keep after
the wedding.

These arrangements will keep young bridesmaids happy on two counts; first they're easier to carry than posies and second the simple bright colours are such fun – sunshine yellow roses and lime-green fennel in a basket stained orange-red.

1 Soak the plastic foam in water, cut it to wedge in the basket.(If you are using a shallow basket, you may need to secure the foam in place with florist's adhesive tape.)

2 Clean the leaves from the bottom 3 cm (1½ in) of the birch stems, then arrange them in the plastic foam creating an even domed outline.

3 Cut the roses and fennel to a stem length of 8 cm (3¼ in) and distribute them evenly throughout the birch stems.

4 Tie a raffia bow at the base of the handle on both sides and trim to complete the display.

YELLOW ROSE
BRIDESMAID'S POSY
• • •

A posy made from slim-stemmed materials has a narrow binding point which makes it easier to carry. This posy uses such materials in a simple but striking combination of yellow roses, lime-green fennel and delicate green birch leaves.

MATERIALS
• • •
20 stems yellow roses
• • •
5 stems fennel
• • •
15 stems birch leaves
• • •
twine
• • •
scissors
• • •
raffia

1 Strip all but the top 15 cm (6 in) of the rose stems clean of leaves and thorns. Split the multi-headed stems of fennel until each stem has one head only. This makes them easier to handle and visually more effective. Strip all but the top 15 cm (6 in) of the birch stems clean of leaves.

Easy to make as a hand-held, spiralled bunch and finished with a natural raffia bow, this posy would be a delight for any bridesmaid to carry and enjoy.

2 Holding one rose in the hand, add individual stems of fennel, birch and rose in a continuing sequence, all the while turning the bunch to spiral the stems. Continue until all the materials are used.

3 Tie the posy with twine at the point where the stems cross – the binding point. Trim the bottom of the stems to leave a stem length of approximately one-third of the overall height of the finished display.

4 Complete the posy by tying raffia around the binding point and finishing with a bow. Finally, trim the ends of raffia.

CELEBRATION TABLE DECORATION

· · ·

MATERIALS

· · ·

*plastic foam ring,
40.7 cm (16 in) diameter*

· · ·

scissors

· · ·

12 stems Senecio laxifolius

· · ·

15 stems elaeagnus

· · ·

3 groups 2 chestnuts

· · ·

.71 wires

· · ·

thick gloves

· · ·

18 stems yellow roses

· · ·

10 stems cream-coloured
Eustoma grandiflorum

· · ·

10 stems solidago

· · ·

10 stems dill

*The arrangement is based on
a circular, plastic foam ring
with the centre left open to
accommodate the wine cooler.
The splendid silver wine cooler
is enhanced by the beauty of
the flowers, and in turn its
highly polished surface reflects
the flowers to increase their
visual impact.*

A table for any celebratory lunch will not usually have much room to spare on it. In this instance there is no room for the wine cooler, and the answer is to incorporate this large, but necessary piece of catering equipment within the flower arrangement.

The floral decoration is a sumptuous, textural display of gold, yellow and white flowers with green and grey foliage. The spiky surfaces of the chestnuts add a wonderful variation in texture.

1 Soak the plastic foam ring in water. Cut the senecio to a stem length of around 14 cm (5½ in) and distribute evenly around the ring, pushing the stems into the plastic foam, to create an even foliage outline. Leave the centre of the ring clear.

2 Cut the elaeagnus to a length of about 14 cm (5½ in) and distribute evenly throughout the senecio to reinforce the foliage outline, still leaving the centre of the plastic foam ring clear to eventually accomodate the wine cooler.

3 Double leg mount three groups of two chestnuts on .71 wire and cut the wire legs to about 6 cm (2¼ in). Take care, as the chestnuts are extremely prickly and it is advisable to wear heavy duty gardening gloves when handling them.

4 Still wearing your gloves, position the groups of chestnuts at three equidistant points around the circumference of the plastic foam ring, and secure by pushing the wires into the plastic foam.

5 Cut the rose stems to approximately 14 cm (5½ in) in length and arrange in staggered groups of three roses at six points around the ring, equal distances apart, pushing the stems firmly into the plastic foam.

6 Cut stems of eustoma flowerheads 12 cm (4¾ in) long from the main stem. Arrange the stems evenly in the foam. Cut the stems of solidago to a length of about 14 cm (5½ in) and distribute throughout. Finally cut the stems of fennel to about 12 cm (4¾ in) long and add evenly through the display, pushing the stems into the plastic foam.

This magnificent arrangement would make a stunning centrepiece for a wedding table.

DRIED FLOWER GARLAND
HEADDRESS
• • •

MATERIALS

• • •

scissors

• • •

9 dried peonies with leaves

• • •

27 dried red roses

• • •

.71 wires

• • •

.38 silver wires

• • •

.32 silver reel (rose) wire

• • •

*27 slices preserved (dried)
apple*

• • •

18 short sprigs dried ti tree

• • •

9 small clusters hydrangea

• • •

*florist's tape
(stem-wrap tape)*

*An advantage of using dried
materials is that they can be
made well in advance, which
means less to worry about on
the big day. There is plenty of
wiring involved, but otherwise
the construction is relatively
straightforward.*

This wedding headdress is made from dried materials in beautiful soft pale
pinks, greens and lilacs with the interesting addition of apple slices. Apart
from being very pretty, it will not wilt during the wedding and can, of course, be
kept after the event.

1 Cut the peonies and the roses to a stem
length of 2.5 cm (1 in). Double leg
mount the peonies with .71 wires and the
roses with .38 silver wires. Group the roses
into threes and bind together using the .32
silver reel (rose) wire. Group the apple
slices into threes and double leg mount
them together with .71 wire. Cut the
sprigs of ti tree, hydrangea clusters and
eucalyptus to lengths of 5 cm (2 in) and
double leg mount with .38 silver wires,
grouping the ti tree and eucalyptus in twos.
Cover all the wired stems with tape.

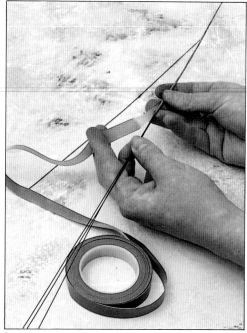

2 Have to hand the bride's head
measurements. Make the stay wire on
which the headdress will be built with .71
wires, ensuring its final length is
approximately 4 cm (1½ in) longer than
the circumference of the head.

3 Position a piece of
wired eucalyptus on
one end of the stay wire
and wrap florist's tape
(stem-wrap tape) over its
stem and the stay wire, to
secure them together.
Then, in the same way,
add in turn a hydrangea
cluster, a group of roses, a
peony and a group of ti
tree, repeating the
sequence until the stay
wire is covered.
Remember to leave the
last 4 cm (1½ in) of the stay
wire uncovered.

4 To complete the
  headdress, overlap the
uncovered end of the stay
wire with the decorated
start and tape together
with florist's tape (stem-
wrap tape), ensuring the
tape goes under the flowers
so that it is not visible.

*The bold nature of this
headdress makes it particularly
suitable for a bride.*

DRIED POMANDER

. . .

*This pomander is time
consuming to build, but will
last. Sprinkle pot pourri
oil over it to provide a
continuing aroma.*

A pomander is generally defined as a ball of mixed aromatic substances. However, this pomander is designed more for its visual impact than its scent. It would look particularly attractive if carried by a bridesmaid. Alternatively it can be hung in the bedroom, perhaps on the dressing-table.

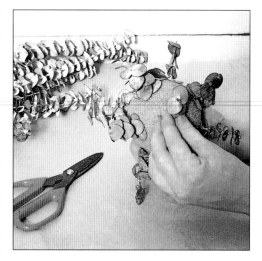

1 Cut the eucalyptus stems into approximately 10 cm (4 in) lengths. Make sure that the stem ends are clean and sharp, and carefully push them into the plastic foam, distributing them evenly over its surface.

2 Cut a length of ribbon long enough to make a looped carrying handle. Make a loop in the ribbon and double leg mount the two cut ends together on .71 wire. Push the wire firmly into the plastic foam ball to form the carrying handle.

3 Cut the stems of the dried roses to approximately 4 cm (1½ in) and wire individually with .71 wire. Group together in threes and bind with .38 silver wire and cover with tape. Cut the dried peony stems to approximately 4 cm (1½ in) and wire them individually on .71 wire, then tape. Wire the dried apple slices individually on .71 wire.

4 Push the wired peonies into the plastic foam, distributing them evenly all over the ball. Push the wired apple slices into the foam, also distributing them evenly over the ball.

5 Push the ten groups of wired roses into the foam, distributing them evenly all over. Cut the ti tree stems into 9 cm (3 in) lengths and push into the foam to fill any gaps around the ball. Once completed you may wish to gently reposition individual elements in order to achieve the most pleasing effect.

Younger bridesmaids may find this charming ball easier to carry than a posy.

DRIED FLOWER CORSAGE

. . .

MATERIALS

. . .

scissors

. . .

2 dried peonies

. . .

3 dried peony leaves

. . .

.71 wire

. . .

.38 silver wire

. . .

3 slices preserved (dried) apple

. . .

3 sprigs dried ti tree

. . .

3 small clusters hydrangea

. . .

8 dried roses

. . .

*3 short stems preserved
(dried) eucalyptus*

. . .

raffia

. . .

*florist's tape
(stem-wrap tape)*

. . .

.32 silver reel (rose) wire

*As an alternative to wearing
the corsage, it could be attached
to a handbag or a prayer book.
Of course, it can be kept after
the event and perfumed with
scented oil*

If dried flowers are the choice for a wedding, a corsage as magnificent as this would be perfect for the mother of the bride. This floral decoration is characterized by softly faded colours in a variety of textures. Dried peonies are used as the focal flowers supported by hydrangeas, roses, ti tree and eucalyptus, and given contrasting textural substance by the unusual addition of preserved apple slices.

1 Cut the peony stems to 4 cm (1½ in) and the three peony leaves to 10 cm (4 in), 8 cm (3¼ in) and 6 cm (2¼ in) respectively. Double leg mount all of these with .71 wire, apart from the shortest peony leaf, which is double leg mounted with .38 silver wire. Double leg mount the apple slices with .71 wire. Cut the sprigs of ti tree to 5 cm (2 in) and form into three small groups, then repeat the process with the hydrangea florets and double leg mount with .38 silver wire.

Cut the rose stems to a length of 2.5 cm (1 in) and the eucalyptus to a length of about 4 cm (1½ in) and double leg mount both on .38 silver wire. Make a small raffia bow and double leg mount on a .38 silver wire around its centre. Tape all of the wired elements with tape ready for making up.

2 Taking the peonies, roses, apple slices and peony leaves, gradually build the arrangement, securing each item individually with .32 silver reel (rose) wire.

3 Position the remaining elements. Attach the raffia bow by its wired stem at the bottom of the arrangement. Secure all materials in place with the .32 silver reel (rose) wire.

4 Trim the ends of the wires to around 6 cm (2¼ in) and cover with tape. You may wish to adjust the wired components to achieve your desired shape.

Dried Rose and Apple Buttonhole

• • •

There are several reasons why dried flowers are preferred for some weddings. This might be because the bride wishes to keep her flowers after the event or it may be a practical measure for a winter wedding where fresh flowers are unavailable or expensive. This buttonhole is designed for a groom or best man and, unusually, incorporates fruit with the flower and foliage.

MATERIALS

• • •

3 slices preserved (dried) apples

• • •

.71 wires

• • •

scissors

• • •

6 dried roses

• • •

.38 silver wire

• • •

*6 short stems glycerined
eucalyptus*

• • •

*1 small head
dried hydrangea*

• • •

florist's tape (stem-wrap tape)

• • •

.32 silver reel (rose) wire

Apple slices give texture and a light touch to the decoration. Add a few drops of rose oil to give scent.

1 Double leg mount the apple slices together on .71 wire. Wire each rose, with a 2.5 cm (1 in) stem, on .71 wire. Double leg mount three roses on .38 silver wire. Leave a 5 cm (2 in) stem on the eucalyptus and hydrangea and double leg mount on .38 silver wire. Tape all the elements.

2 Hold the rose heads in your hand and place the apple slices behind. Then position the hydrangea to the left and bind together all the stems using .32 silver wire. Position the eucalyptus stems to frame the edge of the buttonhole and bind with .32 silver wire.

3 When all these elements are bound securely in place, cut the wired stems to a length of approximately 5 cm (2 in) and bind them with florist's tape (stem-wrap tape). Adjust the wired components to achieve your desired shape, not forgetting the profile.

BRIDE'S VICTORIAN POSY WITH DRIED FLOWERS

· · ·

MATERIALS

· · ·

scissors

· · ·

11 white rose heads

· · ·

18 pink rose heads

· · ·

3 dried pink peony heads

· · ·

.71 wires

· · ·

*12 stems glycerined eucalyptus,
approximately
10 cm (4 in) long*

· · ·

.38 silver wires

· · ·

63 phalaris grass heads

· · ·

*12 clusters dried honesty
with 5 heads
in each cluster*

· · ·

12 small bunches dried linseed

· · ·

*10 small clusters dried
hydrangea*

· · ·

florist's tape (stem-wrap tape)

· · ·

.32 silver reel (rose) wire

· · ·

ribbon

Traditionally the Victorian posy, be it dried or fresh, took the form of a series of concentric circles of flowers. Each circle usually contained just one type of flower, with variations only from one circle to the next. Such strict geometry produced very formal-looking arrangements particularly suitable for weddings.

1 Cut the roses and peonies to a stem length of 3 cm (1⅛ in) and individually single leg mount them on .71 wires. Cut the eucalyptus stems to 10 cm (4 in) and remove the leaves from the bottom 3 cm (1⅛ in), then wire as for roses and peonies.

Double leg mount the phalaris grass and honesty heads on .38 silver wire in groups of five. Single leg mount these groups on .71 wires to extend their stem lengths to 25 cm (10 in). Repeat the process with groups of linseed and hydrangea.

All wired elements should be taped with florist's tape (stem-wrap tape).

2 Hold the central flower, a single white rose head, in your hand and arrange the three peony heads around it, then bind together with .32 silver reel (rose) wire, starting 10 cm (4 in) down the extended stems. (Remember that the starting point for binding determines the final size of the posy, and all subsequent flower circles must be bound at the same point.)

3 Rotating the growing posy in your hand, form a circle of pink rose heads around the peonies and bind to the main stem. Around this, form another circle, this time alternating white rose heads and clusters of hydrangea, and bind. Each additional circle of flower heads will be at an increasing angle to the central flower to create a dome shape.

4 Next add a circle of phalaris grass to the posy. followed by a circle of alternating honesty heads and linseed. Bind each circle with .32 silver reel (rose) wire at the binding point.

The design of this bride's posy follows the Victorian method with just a degree of latitude in the content of some circles. Of course, the arrangement is time-consuming to produce, but the reward is a beautiful posy that the bride can keep forever.

5 Finally add a circle of eucalyptus stems and bind. The eucalyptus leaves will form a border to the posy and cover any exposed wires underneath.

6 To form a handle, place the bundle of bound wires diagonally across your hand and trim off any excess wires. Tape with florist's tape (stem-wrap tape) and cover the handle with ribbon.

DRIED GRASS HARVEST SWAG

∙ ∙ ∙

MATERIALS

∙ ∙ ∙

*1 bunch dried, natural
triticale*

∙ ∙ ∙

*1 bunch dried, natural
linseed*

∙ ∙ ∙

1 bunch dried, natural
Nigella orientalis

∙ ∙ ∙

*1 bunch dried, natural
phalaris*

∙ ∙ ∙

scissors

∙ ∙ ∙

.71 wires

∙ ∙ ∙

*1 straw plait, approximately
60 cm (24 in) long*

∙ ∙ ∙

twine

∙ ∙ ∙

raffia

*Although a good deal of
wiring is required for the
construction of this swag, it is
relatively straightforward and
enjoyable to make.*

This harvest swag is a symbolic collection of dried decorative grasses. It relies on the subtlety of colour differences and textural variation in the grasses for its natural, yet splendid, effect.

In a church at harvest time the swag could be hung on a wall, or a series of them could be mounted on the ends of the pews. In the home it could be hung on a wall, or extended to decorate a mantelpiece.

1 Split each bunch of grass into 8 smaller bunches, giving you 32 individual bunches. Cut the stems to approximately 15 cm (6 in) long and double leg mount the individual groups with .71 wires.

2 Start by tying a wired bunch of triticale to the bottom of the plait with the twine. Then place a bunch of linseed above, to the left and slightly overlapping the triticale, and bind this on to the plait with the twine. Follow this with a bunch of *Nigella orientalis* above, to the right, and slightly overlapping the triticale. Finish the sequence by positioning a bunch of phalaris directly above the triticale, slightly overlapping, and bind on with the twine.

3 Repeat this pattern eight times to use all four varieties of grasses, binding each bunch on to the plait with the twine.

4 When all the grasses have been used and the top of the plait reached, tie off with the twine and trim any excess wires.

5 Make a bow from the raffia and tie it on to the top of the decorated plait, covering the wires and the twine.

HARVEST WREATH
· · ·

MATERIALS
· · ·
27 dried sunflower heads
· · ·
71 wires
· · ·
*florist's tape
(stem-wrap tape)*
· · ·
scissors
· · ·
*30 pieces dried fungus
(various sizes)*
· · ·
3 dried corn cobs
· · ·
large vine circlet
· · ·
raffia

Harvest time conjures up images of fruit, vegetables and ears of corn. This wreath of dried flowers has corn cobs as its harvest time reference point, visually reinforced with fungus, a less obvious autumn crop, and sunflowers, which in this form serve as a reminder of summer days gone by.

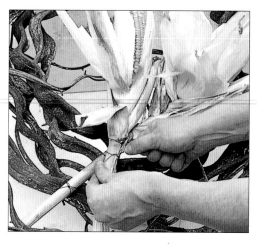

1 Single leg mount individual sunflower heads on .71 wires. Tape the stems, then group in threes. Double leg mount these groups with .71 wire and tape the stems. Double leg mount the pieces of fungus with .71 wire. You may need to cut the wire so that it has a sharp end to push through the fungus and twist into a double leg mount. Do not tape these wires.

2 Group the corn cobs at the bottom of the vine circlet and push their stems between the twisted vines, crossing them over each other to form a fan shape. Secure the corn cobs to each other and to the circlet with .71 wire.

3 Attach the groups of sunflowers, evenly spaced, all around the circumference of the circlet by pushing their wires through and wrapping tightly around the vines. These sunflower groups should alternate between the outside and inside edges of the vines.

4 Attach the fungus in groups of twos and threes around the circlet, between the sunflowers and around the corn cobs. The fungus groups should have the largest piece at the bottom with progressively smaller pieces above. Secure the fungus by straddling the vine with the legs of wire and twisting them together at the back.

5 Finally form a large bow from the raffia and tie it to the wreath over the stems of the corn cobs to conceal any remaining visible wires.

The large scale of this simple but unusual combination of materials gives the wreath great visual impact.

HALLOWEEN DISPLAY
. . .

MATERIALS

. . .

scissors

. . .

*15 slim branches autumn
leaves*

. . .

large ceramic pot

. . .

10 stems Chinese lanterns

. . .

10 stems red hot pokers

. . .

*10 stems orange lilies
'Avignon'*

. . .

20 stems antirrhinum

*This is a fine example of
creating a good shape in a large
display by using the natural
way the material would grow,
and without the support of
plastic foam or wire mesh. The
Halloween atmosphere is
completed by grouping
pumpkins and gourds,
intermingled with candles,
around the base of the
arrangement.*

Make this dramatic arrangement as a decoration for your Halloween party, and, for maximum impact, give it pride of place in a large room or entrance hall. The display is an intriguing mixture of materials in rich autumn colours; long-stemmed, two-coloured antirrhinums, Chinese lanterns, red hot pokers and orange lilies, all set against bright autumn foliage.

1 Cut the ends of the branches of autumn foliage at an angle of 45°, strip the bark from the bottom 5 cm (2 in) and split the branches about 5 cm (2 in) up the stems. Fill the pot with water and arrange the autumn foliage in it to create a fan-shaped outline. This fan must not be flat, and, to give it depth, bring shorter stems of foliage out from the back line into the front and centre of the shape.

2 Strip any leaves from the lower stems of the Chinese lanterns and arrange them throughout the foliage, reinforcing the overall shape. Distribute the red hot pokers throughout the display, again, using taller stems at the rear, and ones getting shorter towards the front.

3 The lilies are the focal flowers in this arrangement. Strip the lower leaves and distribute them throughout the display using taller, less open flowers towards the back and more open blooms on shorter stems around the centre and towards the front. Strip the lower antirrhinum leaves and arrange them evenly throughout the display.

CINNAMON ADVENT CANDLE

· · ·

· · ·

*25 medium thickness
cinnamon sticks*

· · ·

*1 candle, 7.5 x 23 cm
(3 x 9¼ in)*

· · ·

raffia

· · ·

scissors

· · ·

*plastic foam ring for dried
flowers, 10 cm (4 in) diameter*

· · ·

.71 wires

· · ·

reindeer moss

· · ·

20 red rose heads

· · ·

florist's adhesive

*As a bonus, the heat of the
flame releases the spicy aroma
of the cinnamon, and the red
roses completes the festive look
of the candle.
Never leave a burning candle
unattended, and do not allow
the candle to burn down to
within 5 cm (2 in) of the
display height.*

Advent candles often have calibrations along their length to tell you how much to burn each day in the countdown to Christmas. This advent candle has a novel way of marking the passage of time: a spiral of 25 cinnamon sticks of decreasing height. Each day the candle is lit to burn down to the next cinnamon stick until finally on Christmas Day it is level with the shortest.

1 Attach the 25 cinnamon sticks to the outside of the candle by strapping them on with the raffia.

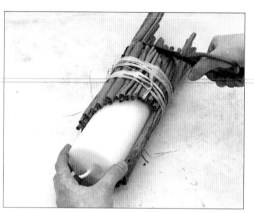

2 Position the cinnamon sticks in equal height reductions so that they spiral around the candle from the tallest at the top to the shortest at the bottom which should be approximately 6 cm (2¼ in) long. The excess lengths of cinnamon will be overhanging the bottom of the candle. Bind the cinnamon securely in place with raffia at two points and cut the excess lengths from the sticks so that they are all flush with the base of the candle.

3 Once the base is level, push the cinnamon-wrapped candle into the centre of the plastic foam ring. Make hairpin shapes from the .71 wires and pin the reindeer moss on to the foam to cover the ring completely.

4 Cut the stems of the dried roses to a length of approximately 2.5 cm (1 in). Add a little glue to the bases and stems of the roses. Push them into the plastic foam through the reindeer moss, to create a ring of rose heads around the candle.

CHRISTMAS ANEMONE URN

· · ·

MATERIALS

· · ·

1 small cast-iron urn

· · ·

cellophane (plastic wrap)

· · ·

1 block plastic foam

· · ·

florist's adhesive tape

· · ·

scissors

· · ·

*1 bunch laurustinus
with berries*

· · ·

10 stems bright orange roses

· · ·

*20 stems anemones
('Mona Lisa' blue)*

*The classic feel of a Christmas
arrangement is retained by the
use of the rusting cast-iron urn
in which this spectacular
display is set.*

This vibrant display uses fabulously rich colours as an alternative to the traditional reds and greens of Christmas. An audacious combination of shocking orange roses set against the vivid purple anemones and the metallic blue berries of laurustinus makes an unforgettable impression.

1 Line the urn with the cellophane (plastic wrap). Soak the plastic foam in water and fit it into the lined urn, securing with the adhesive tape. Trim the cellophane around the rim of the urn.

2 Clean the stems of laurustinus and evenly arrange in the plastic foam to create a domed, all-round foliage framework within which the flowers will be positioned.

3 Distribute the roses, the focal flowers, evenly throughout the foliage, placing those with the most open blooms about two-thirds of the way up the arrangement, and more closed blooms towards the top.

4 Push the stems of anemones into the plastic foam amongst the roses, spreading them evenly throughout the arrangement so that a domed and regular shape is achieved.

TULIP AND HOLLY WREATH

· · ·

*The tulip stems are pushed
fully into the foam in tight
masses, so that only their heads
are visible.*

The extravagant use of white tulips achieves a sophisticated purity in this Christmas decoration. A cushion of white blooms interspersed with glossy dark green leaves and vibrant red berries produces a wreath that can be used either on a door or, with candles, as a table centrepiece.

1 Soak the plastic foam ring in water. Cut the tulips to a stem length of approximately 3 cm (1⅛ in). Starting at the centre, work outwards in concentric circles to cover the whole surface of the plastic foam with the tulip heads.

2 Cover any exposed foam and the outside of the ring with holly leaves by pushing their stems into the foam and overlapping them flat against the edge of the ring. (You may wish to secure the leaves with .71 wire.)

3 Cut 12 stems of berries approximately 4 cm (1½ in) long and push them into the foam in two concentric circles around the ring, one towards the inside and the other towards the outside. Make sure no foam is still visible.

CHRISTMAS CAKE DECORATION

• • •

If you're tired of decorating your Christmas cake in the same old way, with tinsel-edged paper, robins and snowmen stuck on top, be brave and go all out for a whole new look using natural materials! Combined with night-lights (tea-lights), this arrangement forms a memorable Christmas display.

MATERIALS

• • •

*ribbon (width approximately
7.5 cm/3 in) in 2 patterns*

• • •

*3 10 cm (4 in) diameter
Christmas cakes*

• • •

clear adhesive (sticky) tape

• • •

scissors

• • •

gold twine

• • •

1 glass cake stand

• • •

1 handful cranberries

• • •

1 handful small cones

• • •

4 purple tulip heads

• • •

7 red rose heads

• • •

1 stem small camellia leaves

• • •

gold dust powder

• • •

3 night-lights (tea-lights)

Rather than one large cake this display uses a group of three small cakes which themselves become part of the decoration. The rich reds and purples of the flowers and fruit with green and gold trimmings combine lusciously with the night-lights (tea-lights). Never leave burning candles unattended.

1 Wrap the ribbon around the outside of each of the cakes and secure with a piece of clear adhesive tape. Tie the gold twine around the middle of each cake, over the ribbon, finishing with a bow at the front. This is both decorative and useful as it will hold the ribbon in place until the cakes are to be eaten.

2 Position the cakes on the stand and scatter cranberries and cones between them. Pull the petals from the tulips and the roses and scatter them among the cranberries and cones. Scatter camellia leaves similarly. Sprinkle a little gold dust powder over the petals and place the three night-lights (tea-lights) between the cakes.

CLEMENTINE WREATH

• • •

MATERIALS

• • •

.71 wires

• • •

27 clementines

• • •

*plastic foam ring, approximately
30 cm (12 in) diameter*

• • •

pyracanthus berries and foliage

• • •

ivy leaves

*The wreath will look
spectacular hung on a door or
wall, and can also be used as a
table decoration with a large
candle at its centre, or perhaps
a cluster of smaller candles of
staggered heights. The wreath
is very easy to make, but it is
heavy and if it is to be hung
on a wall or door, be sure to fix
it securely.*

This festive Christmas wreath is contemporary in its regular geometry and its bold use of materials and colours. Tightly-grouped seasonal clementines, berries and leaves are substituted for the traditional holly, mistletoe and pine. The wreath has a citrus smell, but can be made more aromatic by using bay leaves and other herbs instead of ivy.

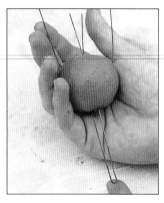

1 Push a .71 wire across and through the base of the clementine from one side to the other, and bend the two projected ends down. Bend another .71 wire to form a hairpin shape and push the ends right through the middle of the clementine so that the bend in the wire is sitting flush with the top of the fruit. Do the same to all the clementines. Cut all the projecting wires to a length of approximately 4 cm (1½ in).

2 Soak the plastic foam ring in water. Arrange the wired clementines in a tight circle on the top of the plastic ring by pushing their four projecting wire legs into the foam. Form a second ring of clementines within the first ring.

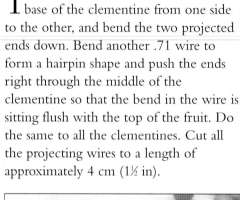

3 Cut the pyracanthus into small stems of berry clusters and foliage approximately 6 cm (2¼ in) long. Push the stems into the outer side of the plastic ring and between the two rings of clementines, making sure it is evenly distributed.

4 Cut the ivy leaves into individual stems measuring approximately 7 cm (2¾ in) in length. Push the stems of the individual leaves into the plastic ring, positioning a leaf between each clementine.

MISTLETOE KISSING RING

· · ·

MATERIALS

· · ·

scissors

· · ·

*7 berries-only stems of
winterberry*

· · ·

large bunch mistletoe

· · ·

twine

· · ·

1 twisted cane ring

· · ·

*1 roll tartan
(plaid) ribbon*

*Very simple in its construction
this design does require a
reasonable quantity of good
quality, fresh mistletoe for it to
survive the full festive season.*

Instead of just tying a bunch of mistletoe to some strategically placed light-fitting in the hall, be creative and make a traditional kissing ring. This can be hung up as a Christmas decoration and still serve as a focal point for a seasonal kiss!

1 Cut the stems of the winterberry into 18 cm (7 in) lengths. Divide the mistletoe into 14 substantial stems and make the smaller sprigs into bunches by tying with twine. Attach a branch of winterberry on to the outside of the ring with the twine. Add a stem, or bunch, of mistletoe so that it overlaps about one-third of the length of winterberry, and bind in place. Bind on another stem of winterberry, overlapping the mistletoe.

2 Repeat the sequence until the outside of the cane ring is covered in a "herringbone" pattern of materials. Cut four lengths of ribbon of approximately 60 cm (24 in) each. Tie one end of each of the pieces of ribbon to the decorated ring at four equidistant points around its circumference. Bring the four ends of the ribbon up above the ring and tie into a bow; this will enable you to suspend the finished kissing ring.

Christmas Candle Table Decoration

• • •

What could be more pleasing at Christmas, when the table is groaning under the weight of festive fare, than to complete the picture with a Christmas candle table decoration?

This rich display is a visual feast of the seasonal reds and greens of anemones, ranunculus and holly, softened by the grey of lichen on larch twigs and aromatic rosemary. The simple white candles are given a festive lift with their individual bows.

MATERIALS

. . .

plastic foam ring,
25 cm (10 in) diameter

. . .

25 cm (10 in) wire basket
with candleholders

. . .

10 stems rosemary

. . .

10 small stems lichen-covered
larch

. . .

10 small stems holly

. . .

scissors

. . .

30 stems red anemones
('Mona Lisa')

. . .

30 stems red ranunculus

. . .

roll paper ribbon

. . .

4 candles

The space at the centre of the design is the perfect spot for hiding those little, last-minute, surprise presents!
Never leave burning candles unattended and do not allow the candles to burn below 5 cm (2 in) of the display height.

1 Soak the plastic foam ring in water and wedge it snugly into the wire basket. You may need to trim the ring slightly, but make sure that you do not cut too much off by mistake.

2 Using a combination of rosemary, larch and holly, create an even but textured foliage and twig outline, all around the plastic foam ring. Make sure that the various foliages towards the outside edge of the display are shorter than those towards the centre.

3 Cut the stems of the anemones and ranunculus to 7.5 cm (3 in). Arrange them evenly throughout the display, leaving a little space around the candle-holders. Make four ribbon bows and attach them to the candles. Position the candles in the holders.

CHRISTMAS TREE DECORATIONS

· · ·

A s an alternative to commercially available Christmas tree decorations why not make your own? The decorations illustrated here use dried flower-arranging materials supplemented with some gold dust powder and seasonal cord and they are so easy to make you can even let the children help you.

MATERIALS

· · ·

FOR STARS AND
CHRISTMAS TREES
1 block plastic foam
(for dried flowers)

· · ·

knife

· · ·

shaped pastry cutters

· · ·

plastic bag

· · ·

loose, dried lavender

· · ·

gold dust powder

· · ·

florist's adhesive

· · ·

loose, dried tulip and rose
petals

· · ·

cranberries

· · ·

gold cord

· · ·

scissors

· · ·

FOR DRIED FRUIT
DECORATIONS
gold cord

· · ·

dried oranges and limes

· · ·

florist's adhesive

· · ·

dried red and yellow rose heads

· · ·

cinnamon sticks

1 For the stars and Christmas tree decorations, cut the block of plastic foam into approximately 3 cm (1 in) thick slices. Using the pastry cutters, press star and tree shapes from the plastic foam. Mix the dried loose lavender with two tablespoons of gold dust powder in a plastic bag (first making sure the bag has no holes in it), and shake together. Liberally coat all the surfaces of the plastic foam shapes with florist's adhesive.

2 Place the adhesive-covered shapes in the bag of lavender and gold dust powder, and shake. The shape will be coated with the lavender heads and powder. As a variation, press some of the dried tulip and rose petals on to the glue-covered shapes before putting them into the bag. Only the remaining exposed glued areas will then pick up the lavender. As a further variation, glue a cranberry to the centre of some of the stars. Make a small hole in the shape, pass gold cord through and make a loop with which to hang the decoration.

3 To make the dried fruit decorations, first tie the gold cord around the fruit, crossing it over at the bottom and knotting it on the top to make a hanging loop. Dab a blob of florist's adhesive on to the base of a rose head and stick it to the fruit next to the knotted gold cord at the top. Dab some adhesive on to two or three short pieces of cinnamon stick and glue these on to the dried fruit, grouping them with the rose head.

CHRISTMAS WIRE-MESH URN
· · ·

MATERIALS
· · ·
scissors
· · ·
15 dried red rose heads
· · ·
.38 silver wire
· · ·
15 heads
Nigella orientalis
· · ·
15 small glycerined beech
leaves
· · ·
75 small pieces cinnamon
stick, approximately 5 cm
(2 in) long
· · ·
gold-coloured cord
· · ·
15 small bunches dried linseed
· · ·
.71 wire
· · ·
florist's tape
(stem-wrap tape)
· · ·
1 wire-mesh urn
· · ·
.32 silver reel (rose) wire
· · ·
dried oranges and limes
· · ·
gold dust powder

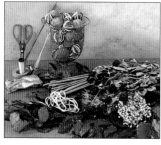

*The urn could be used for all
sorts of Christmas goodies to
brighten a table or sideboard
during the festive season.*

Sometimes we find odd things around the house which, with a little imagination, could be given a new lease of life. In this case an old wire-mesh urn has been turned into a seasonally decorated container for dried fruits.

1 Cut the rose stems and *Nigella orientalis* heads to 2.5 cm (1 in) and individually double leg mount them on .38 silver wires. Stitch wire the beech leaves with .38 silver wires. Tie the cinnamon into groups of five with the gold cord. Push a .38 silver wire around the cinnamon and under the cord. Make 15 bunches of linseed and double leg mount on .71 wires. Tape all the wired materials.

2 Take a bunch of linseed and lay it on the rim of the urn and bind on with .32 silver reel (rose) wire, passing the wire through the gaps in the mesh and pulling it tightly over the wired stem of the linseed and again through the mesh. Attach a rose head in the same way but slightly overlapping the linseed, and repeat this process with the grass head, the beech leaves and the cinnamon bundles.

3 Work continuously around the rim of the urn, always slightly overlapping the materials, until it is covered. Make sure that the materials come together neatly and there is no gap, then stitch the .32 silver reel (rose) wire through the mesh several times to secure finally. Fill the urn with the dried oranges and limes and scatter a little gold dust powder over the whole decoration.

ADVENT CANDLE WREATH
. . .

An Advent wreath has four candles, one to be lit on each of the four Sundays leading up to Christmas Day.
This one is built on a pine foliage ring and uses fruits and spices for its decoration.

1 Attach the four candles at equal distances around the circumference of the ring by cutting away some of the pine needles, putting hot glue on both the base of the candle and on the ring and pressing the two surfaces together for a few seconds. At the base of each candle glue an arrangement of the various materials. The orange slices and cinnamon sticks should be used in groups for the greatest effect.

MATERIALS
. . .
30 cm (12 in) blue pine foliage ring
. . .
45 x 30 cm (2 x 12 in) candles
. . .
scissors
. . .
glue gun and glue sticks
. . .
12 slices dried orange
. . .
4 fresh clementines
. . .
6 dried cut lemons
. . .
5 dried whole oranges
. . .
4 fir cones
. . .
4 physallis heads
. . .
16 short pieces cinnamon stick
. . .
ribbon
. . .
.71 wires

2 Make sure each candle has a selection of the materials at its base, spreading out around the ring.

3 Make four bows from the ribbon and bind with .71 wires at their centres. Attach these to the Advent wreath by pulling the two tails of .71 wire around the width of the ring, twisting them together underneath and returning the cut ends into the moss. Position one bow at each of the four central points between the candles. Make sure that the bows do not touch the candles..

This wreath is not complicated to make and can be used as a table decoration or, with ribbons, it could be hung in your hall.
Never leave burning candles unattended.

GILDED FIG PYRAMID

· · ·

MATERIALS

· · ·

gilded terracotta plant pot

· · ·

*plastic foam cone for dried
flowers, approximately 25 cm
(10 in) high*

· · ·

40 black figs

· · ·

gilding paint

· · ·

.71 wires

· · ·

scissors

· · ·

50 ivy leaves

*This display has a powerful
impact that is disproportionate
to the simplicity of its
construction.*

This abundant use of figs produces a gloriously decadent decoration for a festive table. The deep purple figs with their dusting of gold, arranged with geometric precision, create an opulent yet architectural focal point for the most indulgent of occasions.

1 Make sure that the plastic foam cone sits comfortably in the pot. To ensure stability, you may wish to put a drop of adhesive around the edge of the cone base. Gild the figs slightly on one side of the fruit only, by rubbing the gilding paint on to the skin with your fingers.

2 Wire the gilded figs by pushing a .71 wire horizontally through the flesh approximately 2.5 cm (1 in) above the base of the fruit. Carefully bend the two protruding pieces of wire so that they point downwards. Do take care when wiring the figs or you could tear their skins.

3 Attach the figs to the cone by pushing their wires into the plastic foam. Work in concentric circles around the cone upwards from the bottom.

4 When the cone is covered, position the last fig on the tip of the plastic foam cone, with its stem pointing upwards to create a point.

5 Make hairpin shapes out of the .71 wires and pin the ivy leaves in to the cone between the gilded figs, covering any exposed foam.

INDEX

• • •

Author Acknowledgements

THE AUTHOR WOULD LIKE TO THANK ROGER EGERICKX AND
RICHARD KISS OF DESIGN AND DISPLAY (SALES LTD) FOR THEIR
GENEROUS PROVISION OF FACILITIES

WITH SPECIAL THANKS TO JENNY BENNETT FOR ALL HER HARD WORK.